BOOKS FOR TODAY

The Scurrying Bush

CHARLES SWEENEY

Charles Sweeney was born in Maidenhead in 1922. He served in the R.A.F. during the war and afterwards worked in the Natural History Museum in London. He then went to Africa to do research and study insects. While he was there he started his own zoo—it eventually contained over 200 live exhibits ranging from leopards and hyenas to pigmy-mice and worm snakes—and a museum that housed preserved specimens of some 150 species of the local birds, nearly all species of snakes as well as several thousand insects and other animals.

BOOKS FOR TODAY

Editor: Christopher Parry

THE
SCURRYING
BUSH

CHARLES SWEENEY

CHATTO & WINDUS

LONDON

Published by
Chatto & Windus (Educational) Ltd
42 William IV Street
London WC2

*

Clarke, Irwin & Co. Ltd
Toronto

First published 1966
This edition
first published 1970

SBN 7010 0431 2

Printed in Great Britain by
Butler and Tanner Ltd
Frome and London

To Mother

CONTENTS

ILLUSTRATIONS

Chapter 1

ON THE WING

WHEN I was three I stood up in my cot, stretched out my arms, and said 'I love everybody!' At least, this is one of my mother's favourite stories, and she always shakes her head sadly to think how quickly I was disillusioned for by the age of five it was obvious even to her that I was much more interested in animals than in human beings.

Why this was so I cannot explain. Perhaps because even at this early age I found most people unpredictable whereas an animal nearly always did what was expected. Or perhaps it was my unbounded curiosity together with a well-developed obstinacy. At five I was found half a mile from home wearing my father's hat, with one of his cigars (unlighted and rather crumpled) in one fist, and a large, slimy snail in the other. I willingly relinquished the hat, from under which I could see only by looking down my nose with my head tilted back, and the cigar, the wet taste of which burnt my mouth, but I refused to give up the snail to my captor. I clutched the mollusc firmly as I was led home, and, in spite of all opposition, I kept it in a cardboard box until it died.

From that time onwards nobody could ever persuade me to give up any animal large or small that I wished to keep. After a few battles my parents admitted defeat and made only an occasional protest—when, for example, several white rats escaped, established themselves in our old rambling house and multiplied so excessively that every skirting and crevice seemed to be occupied by pink eyes and quivering whiskers.

Despite this total lack of encouragement from my family, my interest in animals grew as the years passed. When I was nearly seventeen I began to think of my future, but the war shelved this problem for the next five years. My war was more or less uneventful; long stretches of time with few official duties, now and again interrupted by short periods of frenzied activity when we all ran about like ants in a disturbed nest. Fortunately I was posted to small outstations where I could

11

indulge my passion for wild life and the country. Since I was able to find my own billets, I was often lucky. I stayed for a time with a clergyman who was no mean botanist and lent me many of his books—among them *Les Termites* by Hegh which first aroused my interest in African insects.

On another occasion I lived with a skilled poacher in whose home I fed marvellously, although the other conditions were primitive. He taught me much about wild creatures—how to tell the difference between a weasel and a stoat, where to watch the courtship of hares, how to steal upon a sleeping bird and catch it with my hands, and above all how to move silently and observe without being seen. I also remember with affection an old, illiterate woman whose capacity for stout surpassed belief, but whose knowledge of herbs and country lore was such that in an earlier age she would have been regarded as a witch.

Towards the end of the war I was able to pursue more academic studies, and when I was eventually freed I obtained a post in the Entomology Department of the Natural History Museum in London, working for nearly three years in this labyrinthine building. I found museum work very satisfying at first although mine was a junior position; taxonomy interested me, I was able to talk to prominent naturalists, including some of my boyhood heroes. The studious quiet of the Museum, after the muddle of war, seemed to typify the continuity of life, and despite aid-raid damage the institute appeared as permanent and as indestructible as Britain herself.

At the time I felt I wanted no other life, but as the years slipped by I began to realise the limitations of such work. I was fired by a desire to study living examples of some of the strange and wonderful creatures from all over the world that filled cabinet after cabinet, or stared at me in stuffed immobility from walls and alcoves. Daily I examined the pinned insect specimens, especially the tropical ones, so much stranger, more varied, more beautiful, than any our cold climate could produce. I read all I could about them; I listened to naturalists and explorers from abroad, and the more second-hand information I obtained the more obvious it became how comparatively little was known of the lives and habits of many exotic animals. Books contradicted each other and zoologists often disagreed; both were ignorant about much I wanted to know. It seemed that the only way to satisfy my curiosity was to go and see for myself. Africa in particular was my goal, for there not only insects awaited me, but many other interesting animals.

Six months passed and I had no success in finding a job of the sort I wanted — preferably entomological research enabling me to spend my spare time learning something about the other animals. However, just as I was almost resigned to staying in Britain, I was summoned to the telephone one depressing evening in 1949, when the raw cold outside the house seemed to make even the fog swirl and eddy in an effort to keep warm.

It was Dr. Redwood, the head of an English chemical company with a large research department. I had seen him some months previously in the hope that he might be able to offer me a job, for I knew that many of his research staff were seconded to tropical countries for governments unable to maintain permanent specialists; but I had heard no more from him. Now he said that if I were willing to accept immediately he could offer me a post in Tanganyika as a member of a team of three to work on the biology and control of the sisal weevil. I jumped at the offer.

I spent the next three years in East Africa working on this scheme. I was the biologist of the team, my main task to discover as much as possible about the life-cycle, habits and ecology of the weevil, the only serious pest of sisal. Edward was concerned chiefly with insecticide experiments, while Henry investigated the physiology of the plant and kindred matters.

I discovered the weevil to be a dull black insect, about three-quarters of an inch long with a curved snout ending in small but strong jaws with which it chewed the plant. I watched it in the field laying its white eggs in rotting tissue, and followed the life of the larva, which, on hatching, tunnelled in the plant, eventually pupating in a cocoon made from fibres. But to study the life-cycle properly I needed to rear some hundreds of weevils in the laboratory where I could record every detail; Edward also needed thousands to test his insecticides before trying them in the field, and so we offered 50 cents (sixpence) for a hundred adults. This was easy money for the local *totos*, and in a few days, as scores of children, including even those barely able to walk, brought their catch in old tins, grubby pieces of cloth, hollowed out gourds or sisal leaves ingeniously formed into a bag tied with sisal fibres, we found we had far more insects than we needed.

From East Africa, after a few weeks leave, I went to the Sudan on secondment to the Sudan Government. I lived in the Nuba Mountains for five years, being primarily concerned with investigating insect pests of rain-grown cotton, especially cotton stainer bugs, but also advising on many other entomological problems connected with agriculture over an area of thousands of square miles. I left the Sudan in 1956, joining the Overseas Research Service in Britain, and I came to Nyasaland on a cotton pest research scheme, but after three years I resigned to become Government Entomologist, a post I held for the next six years. This job was much wider in scope and therefore more to my liking, and many varied problems came my way—locust swarms, outbreaks of tsetse-fly, hordes of rats, plagues of caterpillars in forests or crops; evicting swarms of angry bees; drafting legislation for controlling imports and exports of agricultural produce to prevent the spread of pests; identifying insects, snakes and other animals connected with suicides, murders and witchcraft; and many other matters that sometimes seemed to have little to do with insects.

*   *   *

Ten days after Dr. Redwood's telephone call I left England by air; 5,000 miles and three days later, I found myself in a much smaller aircraft flying along the coast of Tanganyika on the last lap of my journey. The Indian Ocean was bright cobalt blue with sub-aquatic, emerald-green seaweed masses visible here and there through the clear, smooth water; the bronze of submerged sandbanks gleamed in the white light, while in the distance several islands rose from the sea like mirages in an ocean desert. The deep blues of sky and water merged, so indistinct from one another that a lone cottony wisp of cloud on the horizon seemed to hesitate as though lost. The land was insulated from the water by a narrow strip of sand, dazzlingly white from the air, and broken only occasionally by mangroves or scattered coconut palms. As we turned inland, clean-looking villages of brown, grass-roofed huts sprawled through the green woodland, now and again a roof apparently snow-covered under its burden of drying cassava roots. Pale pencil-like paths wandered drunkenly from village to village through the bushes, stunted trees and graceful palms, the latter so numerous that vast areas seemed to support no other plant life.

The aeroplane suddenly slid sideways, banked steeply, and Tanga was below. Before the aircraft steadied as it came in to land I caught a glimpse of white buildings, a straight road lined with scarlet flame trees, a school and dusty playing field, and rows of russet-coloured, cubical labour lines. A balding grass field edged with twin lines of white dashes rushed towards us; the aircraft bumped violently and slid to a halt in a cloud of choking dust.

As I left the shadow of the plane, the heat from the baking ground made me gasp, the perspiration trickling down my spine before I moved more than a few yards. It was difficult to believe that any animal could survive for long close to that hot soil, but there was plenty of life. Several large grasshoppers rose in front of my feet, brilliant green until they opened their red and purple spotted wings to arch rapidly upwards and as suddenly drop fifty feet away. Some large, shiny black ants stalked deliberately about, apparently oblivious of the heat; I pushed one with my toe and it responded by buzzing loudly and running erratically back and forth in neurotic but ponderous haste. So thick is the armour and so pubescent the body of this large ponerine ant that it is insulated from even the extreme midday heat. Another ant (*Ocymyrmex*), small, brown and thinly armoured, survives the heat in a different manner, and several were speeding so dizzily over the ground on their long legs that they appeared to be flying; they only paused to rest in the shade and I knew that if I held one still on the hot soil for a moment it would die. Bright tiger beetles flew up as quick as startled partridge as I crossed a bare, sandy patch of soil. These, like *Ocymyrmex*, survive because their long legs and rapid movements prevent them being roasted to death.

As I reached the shed, the only building in the field, a praying mantis regarded me with expressionless feline face from the shaded wall, cocking its head to watch me as I passed, and an immense red and black spider hung in an intricate orb-web of strong, bright yellow silk suspended from the overhanging roof. My new colleague greeted me, collected the luggage, and ushered me into the front seat of the black, hearse-like car standing in the meagre shadow cast by the shed. We had a twenty-five-mile drive, he told me, as we bounced away down the corrugated dirt road leaving a trail of dust a hundred yards long.

* * *

That evening, after an early dinner, Edward drove me a few miles to an isolated, empty bungalow. There was heavy, locally made *mvule* and mahogany furniture in the spacious building but nothing else. I had been provided with a camp bed, paraffin lamp and mosquito net.

'You know how to work the lamp all right?' asked Edward, as he prepared to leave.

I nodded, having never seen one before but hoping that I should understand it. At any rate I was not going to admit my ignorance.

'Good. Well, if there's nothing else you want, I'm off. I'll collect you in the morning. Good-night.'

My new colleagues had been welcoming but I was not sorry to be alone again, the first time for four days. It was very hot as I set up my camp bed on the open veranda, and the air was still and heavy. I had some trouble with the lamp, for a two-foot-high flame leapt up like a genie when I first lighted it. However, I subdued it in the end, and left the smoky lamp in the middle of the room. In the bathroom I stripped and washed away the dust of the day by the light of my torch, but the tepid brown water that came from the shower had little power to refresh. An old friend lived in the bathroom—a tiny black ant (*Paratrechina longicornis*) with very long antennae, nesting in a hole in the plaster. This was one of the ants, originating it is thought in South America, that has survived and multiplied in suitable places over the greater part of the world. The last time I had seen it was in the propagating pits in Kew Gardens, and for a minute it reminded me of England.

From the bathroom I could hear the hissing of the lamp, and a number of strange thuds and drones. Wrapping a towel round my waist, I went back to find the air filled with a kaleidoscopic host of insects attracted by the lamp, more living insects than I had ever seen before at one time.

Moths fluttered in their hundreds, varying in size from enormous bat-like emperor moths, with vivid, eyed roundels on the patterned forewings, to a minute, delicate green moth only half the size of a sepal of a daisy; cockchafers zoomed in concentric circles around the lamp, only to break off suddenly from orbit as they neared the light to drop with accelerated speed and thud against the glass. There followed a brief moment of hapless leg-kicking before they righted themselves and took off to repeat the whole performance. Great droves of tissue-soft termites danced falteringly like small opaque ghosts, and amongst them, several brownish flies, each about the size of a bluebottle, methodically hunted the fragile creatures.

Entranced, I stood and watched, now and again brushing off a blundering insect. Apart from the hissing lamp, there was only the noise of insects, and I was surprised by the sounds they made. The noisiest by far were hard-bodied cockchafers and dung beetles, a giant click beetle over three inches long, two fearsome kinds of longicorn beetles with massive jaws, and the horde of male driver ants. They all bumbled about and the vibrations of their wings, their passage through the air and the way they continually collided with obstacles to fall sprawling to the floor, was like a miniature air-raid carried out by suicide pilots.

The male driver ants interested me greatly. These inch-long insects are often called sausage flies or doodle bugs, but comparatively few people seem to realise that they are the male form of the notoriously fierce driver or safari ants. The sausage fly is usually regarded as a kind of wasp, and even those who know that it is an ant, often think that it can bite and sting — not surprisingly, for this sausage-shaped insect buzzes loudly in flight, carries prominent, sickle-formed mandibles, and, if picked up, curves its abdomen as though trying to sting. Unfortunately for the ant it has no weapons, since the seemingly formidable mandibles are useless, and it has long lost the power to sting. Apart from the hard shell and speedy flight, its only protection is a repellent smell.

In some kinds of driver ants the odour is quite strong, in others it is mild. That night, when examining some of the ants,

B

I smelled this scent for the first time. Even when hundreds of the ants are present the smell is not usually very noticeable unless one of the creatures is held close to the nose, but if many of the insects are handled the oily, musty odour will cling to the fingers for some time. Very few of the billions of whizzing males produced each year survive for long; hardly any comes to mate with the wingless, sluggish, sac-bodied female that is so rarely seen.

Worse than the smell of the drivers was the stench of frying insects. Some of the host dropped on the hot lamp to be frizzled in a moment, the pile of burnt corpses producing an unpleasant rancid smell. But the most obnoxious stink of all, an effective deterrent to many potential predators, was that produced by various kinds of living shield bugs. Almost all the members of this and allied families of bugs produce a nauseating, volatile oily secretion that is sometimes so strong that it pollutes the air for yards around. On this night there were only a few stink bugs; I picked up a black one, only to drop it almost immediately as it released its powerful, revolting stench. Although I washed my hands, the offensive smell clung to them for a long time afterwards.

Most of the common shield or stink bugs are eaten by negroes, and later, in the open-air markets in villages, I saw various kinds for sale. When they are roasted the terrible smell disappears and, as do so many other insects, they make a crunchy addition to a diet invariably poor in protein. I have sampled many insects since I lived in Africa; some had little taste, a few were pleasant, but I have never yet eaten a shield bug, being unable to overcome my dislike for the smell.

Apart from the volume of sound produced by the insects round my lamp, I was interested in the variety of sounds produced. One large black ant, for example, the winged sexual form of the one I had encountered at the airstrip that morning, made when I touched it a grating, buzzing noise that could be heard six or seven feet away. A dung beetle rasped in such apparent anger that I could almost sense its grumpiness at being molested; a longicorn beetle produced a shrill note audible at a distance of several yards. All these voices, if amplified, would have rivalled a menagerie of the most vocal mammals.

Such calls are produced by stridulation, by the friction of one hard part of the body moving with great rapidity over another. The songs of grasshoppers, crickets and other *Orthoptera* are as readily recognisable as those of birds, and many other insects stridulate, even some moths. However, not all insect sounds are produced in this manner. Bees, flies and many beetles, such as the cockchafers round my lamp, produce a humming, buzzing or droning sound due to the vibration of their wings as they fly.

Cicadas, unlike other insects, produce their call by means of two special, drum-like organs situated at the base of the abdomen and vibrated by the extremely rapid movements of powerful muscles. Normally cicadas are not much attracted to light, but occasionally one blunders along, and I caught one near the lamp, holding it in my hands. The shrill, one-note calls of many male cicadas (the females are silent for once) are probably the loudest sounds in the insect world, being almost unbearable at close quarters. There are well over 1,000 different kinds of cicada known, some producing little sound, but I held one of the noisier species: its body quivered from end to end like a ship at full speed with the effort of producing its call. I carefully opened my hands and gripped it gently by the body so that the wings were free. Immediately it stopped vibrating, and the tough, membraneous wings began to flutter, gathering speed, until they moved so fast that they appeared to be still, and the whirring they made caused almost as much sound as the insect's whistle.

I released the insect, and it left my hand with astonishing speed. A cicada in flight is one of the world's fastest insects, some species attaining a speed of 60 m.p.h. or more. I watched the squat, streamlined body circle the lamp before thudding into the wall with such impact that it seemed impossible for it to live, but it was apparently unharmed.

Where it fell I noticed for the first time a flat ground beetle, half an inch long, scurrying across the floor, and I trapped it with my hand; there was an explosion under my fingers as a tiny but visible cloud of gas arose from the rear of the beetle. Examining my finger tips I found that they were stained brown and felt hot, and I realised that the beetle was a large bombadier, a member of a group of insects which, when molested, release as a means of defence a puff of caustic secretion like nitric acid. This bombadier was able to discharge several times in succession, after which the supply was exhausted.

I decided to go for a stroll before going to bed. Slipping on a pair of tennis shoes, but not bothering to dress, I picked up my pipe and matches. I thought how strange it was that here was I wandering about clad only in a towel, when only a few days before I had been shivering with cold in a suit and overcoat. Instead of a tarred lamplit pavement between rows of houses, I walked along a track that meandered through rows of young sisal under a sky dark with rolling black clouds, lit only by the faint light of a quarter moon, feeling between my toes the reddish dust that puffed up at every step.

Supposing for some reason I had to leave again to-morrow, I thought, even the little I had seen already had made my journey worthwhile. Africa might be harsh and primitive; hot and dusty, as at present, or humid and oppressive, as it would be later no doubt. A land that from the air looked neat and clean, but was often dirty and untidy, even squalid, in towns and villages; a land with the threat of sinister diseases— malaria, yellow fever, bilharzia, hookworm, elephantiasis, leprosy and scores of others. But a land that promised adventure, including all the wild life that I could wish to see, and I was not going away to-morrow, I was here for at least two years.

I stopped to light my pipe and became aware of the silence, emphasised only by the gruff 'ka-rack, ka-rack' of frogs calling to one another in chorus in the distance, and the faint beat of drums brought by the freshening breeze. By a small acacia bush, I marvelled at the two-inch-long spines and the strange silhouette of the shrub in the fitful moonlight; then I gradually became aware of a curious sound at my feet, like the patter of ink on parchment or the beat of a tiny drum.

At first I thought I must have imagined the noise, but I heard it again, immediately followed by echoes coming from several directions. I could not locate the source. I felt as though I were surrounded by some miniature but invisible army, for despite the smallness of the sounds, they beat a rapid, urgent tattoo. Searching in the light of a match, I found that it *was* an army—an army of termites. Only a few yards away was their home, a craggy mound of red earth, crenulated and turreted like a medieval castle.

The termites (*Pseudocanthotermes militaris*) were working in small parties all round me, foraging for dry grass and leaves under the acacia bush. My approach had disturbed them, and had at once brought their warning system into operation. Those aware of the commotion I had made began to bang their heads rhythmically against the ground, or climbed on a dry leaf and tapped on that; the call was taken up by others and passed on until dozens of termites were drumming in different places. The rest hurriedly, but in good order, headed for their holes and filed down into the ground. In a few moments only the last laggard drummers were to be seen.

Nearly all termites are entirely subterranean, making earthen tunnels over the surface of the soil or on plants when they forage above ground, but this termite looks for its food quite openly at night or on cool, rainy days, relying on the warning system to protect the colony from enemies. The termites make no attempt at concealment, although they work feverishly and take alarm at the slightest vibration on the ground. Their underground tunnels radiate from the nest that lies in and below their castle, each tunnel ending in a small hole at the soil surface from which the insects emerge to scavenge for vegetable matter within a radius of a few yards.

I was just twisting my towel back into position, for it had slipped, when I nearly dropped it altogether as a cheerful shout behind me made me jump. Two shadowy Africans, like disembodied shirts and shorts, their heads and bare limbs indistinct from the night itself, passed by. Clutching my towel rather foolishly, I answered 'Good-night' in English. The animated clothes disappeared into the darkness, and a few heavy drops of rain spilled from the swollen clouds. The air became suddenly chilled, as the wind, sweet-smelling of wet soil, blew lustily at my back. I ran for home, but the rain was quicker. I heard it coming behind, hissing like a steam cock, for a full minute before it overtook me, and I reached the bungalow gasping and shivering from the shock of the cold, bucketing downpour.

By the time I had dried myself on my only remaining towel, there was a big puddle of rain in the centre of my bed in which a water beetle was already swimming madly round and round.

Chapter 2

MKULUMUZI GORGE

MOST of my work was based at my field laboratory some twenty-five miles from the research station where I lived, and I travelled there and back along an unsurfaced earth road, very dusty in the dry weather, very muddy in the rains, and at times impassable. Edward and Henry carried out most of their research on the station, so I did not see them very often.

At the field laboratory I employed some dozen men, optimistically called 'laboratory assistants'. There were many eager applicants for these jobs when I started work, for they were considered to be superior posts, conferring a high social standing. Of course none of these recruits had any experience, so I was forced to choose my staff almost at random and not all were a success. I wanted the men to make simple counts of insects in the field, and those eventually selected were taught to recognise various insects, and to help in uncomplicated field experiments.

Most of these men (or rather boys, since none was more than about twenty years of age) just carried out the work for which they were employed, but four of them were my companions on many occasions unconnected with my official research.

Kazimoto, one of the first I employed, became more of a friend than an employee. He was from the south; very black, tall, strong, generally good-natured, dignified in spite of his twenty years, and with a sense of humour but not a very strong personality. His greatest asset was his common sense. If he did not understand an instruction, he said so, and, as most people who have dealt with junior African employees will admit, this is a rare characteristic indeed. His formal education, to a western mind, anyway, was sketchy; he could read Swahili and write after a fashion; he knew some elementary arithmetic and he was able to count in English. In common with all the Africans I employed at the field laboratory, he knew little English, but this was an advantage as it forced me to learn Kiswahili.

23

Kazimoto's ability to think straightforwardly about a problem, and his honesty of mind were attributes to be envied notwithstanding his great ignorance, and he very soon became my head assistant. On leaving Tanganyika I did my best to take him with me to the Sudan, but it proved impossible. I found him a good job in Kenya, however; he is still there having become a botanist with a private firm.

Jonipayo was a strange character with a much lighter skin than most Bantu negroes. He said that he was a Barotse from Northern Rhodesia, which was probably true, but I think that he had some Arab blood in him, perhaps from a great-grandparent. Standing about five and a half feet, he was so slight and wiry with a build more like that of an Indian than an African, that he seemed even shorter. Although uneducated, he had acquired a certain sophistication for he was a travelled young man having worked for short periods in Salisbury, Johannesburg and other cities. He was in strong demand as a dancer and had a great reputation as a witchdoctor. He taught me the Swahili names of many plants and the uses of certain herbs. If I said to any of the others 'What is this plant called? What is the name of that bird?' the invariable answer was an apathetic 'Sijui' ('I don't know'). Anything that was regarded as inedible or useless was at best ignored, but superstitious fears caused many harmless creatures to be killed. Jonipayo at least added to his store of knowledge, and was genuinely interested in some of the facts I was able to tell him.

All the same Jonipayo's disposition was a happy-go-lucky one; I liked him and he trusted me up to a point, but he was an incorrigible liar, quarrelsome when drunk, and had as little respect for private possessions as would be expected of someone brought up in a primitive society where most property is communal.

The other two boys were more ordinary, although Atanazi looked villainous enough to stand out in any crowd. He was not tall but muscular and thick-set, his face disfigured by two tribal scars on the cheek, and these, together with his purplish thick lips, small, narrow eyes, lowering forehead and a nose squashed so flat that it was broader than long, gave him a most evil appearance. Dressed in a leopard skin, brandishing a spear, he would have been the very personification of a primitive savage, but as a matter of fact, although taciturn, he was gentle and something of a dandy. His success with the girls was phenomenal although he was scarcely eighteen, and he was continually in trouble with irate husbands and scandalised fathers. Apart from his conquests, he appeared to have no other interests or ambitions.

Felici was probably the youngest of the four. He was even more of a dandy than Atanazi having a great love for flamboyant shirts and ties. Whatever garish colour scheme he flaunted, however, he always looked clean and neat. He was a local boy, good-humoured, well-built, with a round, full face, but rather timid. Although he was liable to take offence and sulk at real or imagined snubs, he and I got on well. He was rather better educated than the others, intelligent and mildly ambitious, but without the perseverance to fulfil many of his hopes. I could never give him any position of authority over the other men in spite of his greater learning, for he was too young and, with any encouragement, became unbearably swollen-headed.

When the time came for me to leave Tanganyika, Jonipayo was in prison for three months for knifing another man in a drunken brawl at a beer-dance; I went to the prison a few days before I left to pay him some money and he was his usual cheerful self. I asked him how he was.

'Fine, *Bwana*,' he said. 'There's plenty of food, I have been given these clothes and I live here for nothing.'

Obviously he was enjoying his stay at 'King Georgis Hotel'. I did not hear of him after he was released except that he had left the area, it being rumoured that he had gone to Kenya to try his luck there. Felici and Atanazi found other jobs locally.

*   *   *

After I had settled down in my new work and home, I found interest almost everywhere close by, for there were always new insects to watch, strange plants to examine, and often animals to see—occasionally larger mammals, such as lion, leopard, duiker, wild pig and bushbuck.

Some of the wildest, most fascinating country in the region was to be found only a few miles from my field laboratory. The Mkulumuzi River flowed through this area which was for the most part uninhabited and shunned by all the local people apart from a hunter or two in the dry season. It was only a small, muddy stream that sluggishly entered the Indian Ocean just north of Tanga; occasionally, for a few hours or days in the rains, injected with new life, it would roar and tumble fast-flowing with white-flecked surface like a grown-up river. The Mkulumuzi was especially attractive to me for it flowed through a wild limestone gorge where many caves and pot-holes were to be found. Although only a few miles from urban development and of course not unknown country, to me the Mkulumuzi region was as intriguing as the remotest parts of the tropical world.

I discovered the gorge when I went with some friends to visit the so-called Amboni Caves, a tourist attraction a few miles from Tanga. Here the local villagers took us round the two show-caves, lighting our way with flaring, smoky torches made from dry, tightly twisted grasses. In and around the two caves were the initials or names of visitors scratched, chiselled and sometimes even painted on the rock surface (do some people carry small pots of paint about with them to try and perpetuate their memory?). The rubbish of civilisation lay scattered everywhere. Even the bats had deserted these two caves. I never returned to them, but I realised that they formed the extreme end of a very considerable limestone system that probably extended for miles upstream, and I determined to investigate the river gorge as soon as I could.

I asked Felici and Juma, both locals, about the Mkulumuzi Gorge.

'Nobody ever goes there,' said Felici, 'it is wild country; there are no tracks, the bush is so thick that even in the dry season it is impossible to pass through. You can't go there, *Bwana*.'

Juma was even more vehement. 'There are many leopards and other fierce animals, and sometimes the spirits take the shape of such beasts. It is a most evil place. The Great River Spirit himself lives there in a cave. Nobody can go there,' he repeated.

'How do you know all this if nobody has ever been there?' I asked.

Juma said that his uncle had hunted there a few years ago

but one moonlit night he had met a spirit in the guise of a giant leopard that had threatened to kill him if he ever went there again. 'My uncle told me about this place,' Juma concluded. Felici said that he had heard about the river valley from the old ones of his village, but he had never been there himself.

'Well, come with me on Saturday,' I said, 'you and Juma and Kazimoto.'

*   *   *

Saturday came. Juma politely but firmly refused to come. He was not going to anger the spirits of the river. In the end, Kazimoto, Jonipayo and, rather reluctantly, Atanazi and Felici, went with me.

Instead of approaching the gorge from Amboni I drove from my laboratory to the extreme boundary of the sisal estate. I intended to cut through the bush at right-angles to the Mkulumuzi which, according to my calculations, flowed some two miles off. I meant to search some of the caves and to discover if any animals lived in them.

Leaving the car, we entered the bush following an animal track that seemed to lead in the right direction. A party of red-billed hornbills flew off, their raucous prolonged clucking calls rising to a mocking crescendo as they disappeared, swooping up and then down behind the tree screen. The tenuous path soon petered out, and for the first time I realised just how dense untouched bush could be. This was not jungle, if by jungle is meant the usual conception of great forest trees on the Amazonian pattern shutting out the sun, for such forests are rare in Africa and found only in very heavy rainfall areas usually at higher altitudes. Nevertheless bush of this kind is just as difficult to penetrate—often more difficult because where there are tall forest trees with a closed overhead canopy the undergrowth is sparse; without such densely growing trees the bush may form an almost solid wall. It is not difficult to walk through a beech or pine wood in England, but a large thicket of blackthorn is nearly impenetrable and offers some comparison with dense African bush. Although most of the bush country of Africa is relatively open, here we were confronted by a tangled wall of green, a dense hedge of great thickness, through which we had to hack our way with *pangas* (broad-bladed, two-foot-long knives).

The region had apparently never been cleared by man, and no fire had been through for many years. Acacias with acicular, two-inch-long spines, or curved needle-sharp thorns, were dominant amongst perhaps a dozen other tree species, mostly as spiny, and the trees were festooned and anchored by a mass of lianas, creepers, climbing spinach and other prickly twiners. If we cut a branch through it remained supported by a dozen strangling creepers, each of which had to be severed before the branch fell. Giant aloes grew below the trees, each leaf edged with hooked spurs. Palm-like plants with serrated, sword-shaped leaves barred our way. Candelabra euphorbia, their green arms stretching skywards like cacti, often hidden by an ambitious riot of lesser foliage, formed the nucleus of many a thicket. Just to bruise one of the soft green limbs of this plant caused the pure white, sticky, poisonous sap to begin to drip. This has no effect on the skin but as we cut our way through we had to be careful to shield our faces for the sap is excruciatingly painful should it enter the eyes. From an insignificant undergrowth weed arose a peculiar smell, like curry-powder, that hung in the still oven-hot air, masking any more agreeable odours there may have been.

It took us nearly an hour to penetrate only a few hundred yards by which time every inch of clothing I wore was saturated with sweat. Little birds flew off at our approach; ahead came the wild, bell-like call of a red and yellow barbet, the first time I had ever heard this unmistakable cry. Just as I was thinking of turning back, the vegetation began to show signs of relenting. Small open patches of ground appeared and the going became easier.

A moment later there was a shout from Felici, who had been leading, and he began to roll on the ground, apparently in great pain. He took no notice of our questions, and I did not know what was wrong with him. Jonipayo came up from behind, however, holding some broad, sappy leaves which he gave to Felici who immediately tore off his clothing and began to rub the leaves vigorously on his body. The others spoke in such rapid Swahili that I could not follow.

'What on earth's the matter?' I asked Jonipayo. I could

not understand all of his reply, but apparently Felici had been 'attacked' by some plant that had set his body 'on fire'.

'Where is it? Show me,' I demanded.

Cautiously Jonipayo parted some leaves and pointed. I saw the innocent-looking brown pods of the buffalo bean or cow itch* hanging from several branches.

The stem of the buffalo bean is thin and twining, usually growing over other plants; when climbing a large tree the beans may have slender branches fifty feet or more in length. I could see the silvery-haired leaves at intervals along the stems, each leaf divided into three leaflets or lobes. Only a few of the large, drooping, dark purple flowers were still present but there were many fruits growing in clusters, each fruit a bean-like pod about three inches in length, the immature fruits smaller, green and hairless, the mature fruits densely covered with velvety brown hairs.

A slight breeze, or any movement of the supporting plant, is sufficient to release numbers of the tiny, rusty brown hairs from the ripe pods, to which they are very loosely attached. Where the hairs settle on the skin an intense and burning irritation is set up, and the effect of large numbers can be most unpleasant and painful. Only the hairs from the ripe beans cause the irritation (young pods are often cooked and eaten); otherwise the plants are quite harmless and as a rule pass unnoticed.

Felici had walked right into a great shower of the hairs which covered him from head to foot, and he must have been in considerable pain. There is little one can do about buffalo bean except wait for the irritation to subside, as it always does eventually, for the various African remedies that I have seen are of little use. Probably Felici's discomfort did not last as long as it might because the streams of perspiration washed the hairs away. Afflicted animals, even men, sometimes roll in mud which as it contracts is said to help pull out the fine hairs. In some places I have seen acre upon acre infested by this

* *Mucuna pruriens:* there are a number of other species, and there seems to be a considerable difference in the irritating properties of the various species and possibly even between different plants of the same kind.

irritating bean, making even open bush almost impenetrable when the fruit are ripe, but in this case we were lucky for there appeared to be only one or two plants with ripe pods.

We skirted round the thicket in which the ripe beans hung, and in a short time the vegetation thinned considerably, and the ground became rockier.

By this time we had climbed to several hundred feet above sea-level; there was still no sign of the river valley, but I thought that we must be getting close. All around us was a wild, strange countryside made up of tumbled, crumbling limestone rocks weathered into the weirdest shapes. Occasionally a fractured rock mass of several tons was half supported by a smooth conical pillar of stone, perhaps not more than two inches in diameter at the top, looking as if a hard push was all that was required to bring it tumbling down. Other erosion had caused flat slabs of rock, often only a few inches in thickness, to cleave and crack so that they jutted from more solid faces to resemble giant pieces of jig-saw puzzles. Outcrops of fantastic designs surrounded us, making grotesque shapes in the intense white glare; some rocks resembled tombstones, others caricatured animals or plants. Stumpy baobab trees, like great grey bottles sprouting numerous arms, grew here and there, adding their touch of unreality to the eerie landscape.

As we carefully traversed the uneven, rocky ground of this wilderness, Felici and Atanazi were startled by every lizard that scuttled away at our approach often dislodging some of the smaller flakes of rock, and we all jumped when a ring-necked dove noisily flapped out from a low bush close by. Even I could imagine this place to be the home of supernatural animals and ghosts. Much of the rock was riddled with holes, caves and crevices, with potholes often forty and occasionally over one hundred feet in depth below our feet, and we had to take care not to slip on the loose, shaly stones.

I had almost given up hope of finding the river when we came to the edge of a cliff. The vegetation on the steep slope was too dense for us to see the bottom, but I felt sure that we had reached the edge of the gorge. The way down was more difficult than the previous part of our journey for the scrambling luxuriance obscured the crumbling limestone cliff face. However, with the aid of a sisal rope, and some stout trees on the cliff, we eventually found ourselves, somewhat scratched and bruised, apparently in the river valley.

The gorge here was probably some eighty yards across but from the midst of the green world in which we found ourselves it was impossible to judge. The river, not being in spate, was only a few feet wide, and flowed invisibly through a living tunnel of plants. Tall, graceful *Mfune** trees lifted their heads seventy or a hundred feet above the rabble below in a gracious umbrella of branches. Here and there an *Mvule*† tree soared upwards out-topping the *Mfune*, the smooth, sheer trunks branchless for the first sixty or seventy feet. Great burly figs seemed to be wrestling like Laocoon with serpentine lianas, some as thick as a man's thigh, while a ravelled skein of plants surged round their feet. Delicate *Combretum* trees struggled for life, and gnarled and rugged *Grewia* bushes sent scandent spears through the green wall around them. Where the trees and shrubs left room, grasses grew twelve feet or more in height.

In this vegetable chaos we had to hack a way through with *pangas* in order to struggle over the top of the cut branches, scarcely setting foot on the ground. Fortunately we came now and again to open spaces where the ground was too rocky for many plants to gain a foothold, and near the cliff bottom the fallen scree was almost devoid of plants. Keeping close to the cliff, we progressed some two hundred yards along the valley before we found the first cave entrance.

'Bring the lamp,' I told Kazimoto, 'we'll look in here.' The lamp was still intact as it had been firmly packed in a box carried by Kazimoto. I now had some difficulty in calming the fears of my companions. They had come so far with little demur, but now that I was preparing to enter a cave, they had serious doubts. The cave was a place of damp darkness, of mystery and magic, the home of demons, which no sensible person would even consider entering. My motives were completely alien to these men, and even Kazimoto was not very willing to come with me. However, they were persuaded in the end, for it was a choice of two evils as they were almost as afraid to remain where they were.

Passing through a narrow entrance we found ourselves in a
* *Sterculia appendiculata*.   † *Chlorophora excelsa*.

deserted cavern about the size of a large room. From here I led the way along a short tunnel into another, much larger cavern. In the distance we could hear the dripping of water, and, as we stopped and listened, there came another sound. A peculiar noise that could be described only as a kind of reboant, hissing screech, not very loud, but sounding most uncanny in the cool, silent depth of the cavern. It was unlike any earthly cry. Although not powerful, the sound carried and, probably owing to some acoustic property of the cave, we could not locate its direction.

The effect on my companions was immediate. For a second they stood petrified in the restricted circle of lamp-light; then they ran back towards the entrance. The lamp went out as there was a crash of glass, followed by silence.

'Kazimoto! Kazimoto!' I called.

'*Nipo hapa, Bwana,*' came fearfully from close by, for he had not run far. I switched on my electric torch. The strange vibrating noise came again, seemingly from several directions at once. Following the others to the entrance, I was surprised to find them not far away, for I had scarcely expected to see them again that day. Jonipayo came up sheepishly, followed by Felici and Atanazi, when they saw us emerge from the cave. I tried to find out what they thought had caused the noise.

'It is a *pepo*,' said Felici, shivering.

'*Nini hii?* What's a *pepo*? *Niambie,*' I asked, puzzled, for the word was new to me. There was no reply, only an embarrassed silence and scuffling of feet.

'Kazimoto,' I said sternly, '*what* is a *pepo*?'

Most Africans are loath to discuss supernatural happenings of any kind, particularly in such a forbidding place as the gorge, for fear of angering any listening spirits; in this case I had little doubt that even Kazimoto considered the sounds to be of an unearthly origin, and my enquiries to be in bad taste.

Kazimoto hesitated. 'A *pepo, Bwana*?' As though the word were new to him also.

'Yes, that's what I said. Come on, tell me.'

'Well, a *pepo* . . . a *pepo's* a kind of ghost, a *shetani*, a *jini*.'

'Go on.'

'It is evil, *Bwana*,' Kazimoto continued in a whisper, 'it is one that lives in caves and other wild places, and jumps on people causing them to die. We should not talk of it here' (the others murmured agreement, nodding their heads violently) 'although I myself do not believe this sound to have been made by a *pepo*.' The others looked shocked, and uneasily looked about at this heresy. 'It is perhaps only the *pepo's* servant,' Kazimoto went on, rather doubtfully, 'at any rate we saw nothing and we are not dead.'

I could elicit no more information concerning the natural history of *pepos*. When I decided to return to the cave to investigate, Kazimoto begged me not to go inside again. Not long ago, he told me, another *mzungu* (European) went into one of the caves near Amboni at the other end of the gorge, but he never came out again. I never discovered if Kazimoto fabricated this story to dissuade me, but he did stress that the Africans with the European were blamed for letting the white man go by himself. The search party found no trace of the man although the cave was only a small one.

'All Europeans are mad,' muttered Atanazi.

'But some are powerful and know much magic,' said Jonipayo. 'Our *Bwana* knows some magic. He has charms for snakes, look how he can pick them up without dying, and the python is often the servant of the *pepo*, so perhaps he can protect himself.'

Felici suggested that before I went I wrote a note saying that he and the others were not to blame for my folly, for he was convinced that I would never be seen again.

Inside the cave I stopped once more in the same place and listened. For some minutes I heard nothing, and then I heard another sound—this time more like a sharp bark. It seemed to come from another passage ahead that we had not explored. I moved forward quietly, shielding my torch, stopping at almost every step, but I heard no other cry. The tunnel became smaller, and I had to bend double for a few yards before it opened out into a third cavern from which radiated numerous small passages.

Flashing my torch I was in time to see a rodent-like animal disappear through one of the narrow openings. Hurrying across the cavern floor I peered along the passage, but the animal had vanished, and the opening was too small for me to follow.

c

I had only a brief glimpse of the little creature, but it was obviously a hyrax, sometimes called a rock rabbit or dassie. Searching around the cave I soon found the urine-stained rock and pile of black round droppings associated with these animals. The hyrax tends to leave its excrement in one place, usually at a considerable distance from its sleeping quarters, several animals often using the same midden for years. Sometimes very considerable deposits can be found, and at other times I found the droppings three feet or more in depth between rocks. It is strange to think that the faeces of the rock rabbit, like the secretion from the anal gland of the civet, and other animal substances, helps to make the women of 'civilised' countries smell sweeter, for it contains a substance called hyraceum, which is used commercially and incorporated in various perfumes.

It was not until I went to live in the Sudan that I found that the fluid excreta of the hyrax is also employed in the manufacture of cartridges for old flint-lock guns, and even for more modern weapons. The fluid is collected from the midden, boiled in an old *safia* or *debie* (a four-gallon tin originally used for containing petrol or paraffin) for a long time until most of the excess water is evaporated. When dried in the sun, it forms a powder that ignites easily and burns slowly.

I waited for some minutes in the cave to see if any hyrax would return, but none appeared. I investigated each of the narrow passages in turn, but they were all too small for me to enter. As I shone my torch into the fifth tunnel I could see no movement at first and the passage seemed to be as deserted as the others, but, as my eyes adjusted themselves, I distinguished the head of a snake withdrawing almost imperceptibly. The next moment it had disappeared altogether. It was probably a python, but there was something sinister about the silent way this Cheshire Cat of a snake vanished before I could identify it.

There seemed to be no other life in the caves. I waited a further ten minutes but I heard no further noises except the occasional plop of water. There seemed to be no possible cause of the original peculiar sounds that had driven the Africans out of the cave, unless it had been some odd acoustic effect distorting the cry of a hyrax.

As I left the caves I met a very relieved Kazimoto near the entrance of the first cavern. Worried by my prolonged absence he had come to look for me, but the others had refused to accompany him.

'Well, I don't know what made that noise, Kazimoto,' I said, 'but I saw a small animal — I don't know what you call it in Swahili — and, I think, a python. Perhaps the other animal made the noise, but I do not think it was the python.'

'It was the python, *Bwana*. The *pepo's* servant warning us,' Kazimoto said emphatically as we rejoined the others outside the cave, 'we must not go back again.'

The others nodded agreement. The reptile I had seen was certainly a *pepo* in disguise or the *pepo's* servant. Making the difficult journey back to the car, they argued all the way about *pepos* and our 'escape'.

I never discovered to my complete satisfaction the source of the strange sounds, although we returned to this cave many more times, Kazimoto and Jonipayo being by then hardened spelaeologists no longer much worried by *pepos*. Nor did we ever see another python or even a hyrax inside this or any other cave on the Mkulumuzi.

Chapter 3

THE ELEPHANT'S COUSIN

ALTHOUGH the wild Mkulumuzi Gorge and many of the hills abounded with rock rabbits, I only glimpsed them now and again, and it was not until some years later in the Sudan that I was first able to study them properly.

The hyrax is an odd-looking little animal.* The soft fur is grey or greyish-brown with lighter underparts, but the arched back and rounded rump give it the appearance of a hunch-backed, tail-less rat, the tail being all but invisible. Yet the face is not rodent-like and would have a weasely appearance were it not for the round, dark brown but bright, intelligent-looking eyes, for the hyrax has a sharp snout, with the jaws set well back behind the nostrils, and small, rounded ears. Its legs are short, the hind limbs slightly longer than the front limbs, with four fingers but only three toes. While the teeth are similar to those of a rodent, each of the two, large, curved incisors in the upper jaw is sharply pointed instead of being chisel-shaped as in a rat. Probably the most remarkable feature of the hyrax is its foot, however. Each foot has a soft, moist pad which acts as a sucker enabling the animal to cling with ease to vertical rocks and trees.

Although the rock hyrax is only about sixteen inches long and weighs little more than eight pounds when adult, it is not an animal to trifle with, for when cornered it is full of courage. It will stand at bay, dancing and chattering with rage, ready to sink its sharp-pointed fangs in its tormentor if given the slightest chance. One day in the Usambara, collecting insects

* Some twenty-five species of hyrax are known to exist in Africa and parts of Asia, the Coney of the Bible (*Procavia syriaca*) being one kind. The largest species is little bigger than a hare, the smallest the size of a guinea-pig, while most are rabbit-sized. Apart from size, hyraces show little resemblance to the above animals, but are most nearly related to the largest land animal in the world, the elephant, which they resemble in foot and skull structure and other anatomical details. Hyraces are all very similar in appearance, although some live in trees while others prefer rocky hillsides.

36

from a hill top, I saw three dogs, in probably their first encounter with a hyrax, flee howling with fright when pursued by
an old male they had disturbed. One of the flying mongrels left
a scarlet, glistening trail on the rocks from a wound in its
muzzle delivered by the chittering bundle of fur that bounded
like a hairy ball in their wake. Of course, a hyrax at bay is no
match for several experienced dogs under the direction of their
master, but in this case the dogs were from a near-by village,
hunting on their own account.

Occasionally rock rabbits become rabid, picking up the in-
fection when bitten in encounters with dogs, jackals or other
creatures. One rabid animal in the Sudan caused the death of a
villager and his dog before it too succumbed to this terrible
disease. Another attacked me one day when I was collecting
animals on a *jebel* in the Sudan; fortunately I was able to kill it
with a stick before it could bite me or my companions. Although I did not confirm that it was rabid, there is little doubt
that it was, for hyraces normally do not unprovokedly attack
human beings. Rabies is spread only by a bite, and it seems
likely that a rabid hyrax is avoided by the rest and often
wanders away, so that the others are rarely infected. I have
only seen rabid hyraces in the Sudan, but the disease probably
occurs in these animals in other parts of Africa as well.

Apart from the very occasional animal with rabies, or when
acting in self-defence, the rock rabbit is a peaceable and
delightful little creature, although, like human beings, it sometimes becomes cantankerous in old age. It is almost entirely
herbivorous, feeding on the grasses, roots, bulbs, leaves and
shoots of plants in its habitat, sometimes travelling a quarter
of a mile, but rarely farther, from its rocky hideout to devour
the fruits or seeds of a favourite tree in season, but never normally roaming far from its home and, in the case of those I
knew in the Sudan, never descending into the valleys. The
hyrax is a social animal living in colonies consisting of a dozen
to perhaps fifty individuals, or sometimes adjacent colonies of
several hundred may be found.

To watch a colony from some vantage point is an interesting
experience. The animals are only active during the early
morning and late afternoon, or at night, usually on warm,
moonlit nights, the rest of the time being spent in cool retreats

amongst tumbled rocks or caves. In the Sudan there was one
colony I used to watch at frequent intervals.

In the early afternoon, about 2 p.m., I would climb high
into the shimmering hills, where to touch a bare granite rock
with my naked hand would sometimes cause a blister, and
reach a flat-topped boulder shaded by a small mountain fig
under which I could relax. It was an hour's climb to this spot,
and when I arrived it was as though I had emerged from a
river, so saturated and dripping were my clothes. I would
spread my shirt to dry in the sun and mop myself with a towel
before settling down to wait for the hyraces to emerge. From
my rock I could see right across the valley, and, later, as the
sun's rays began to slant and the light softened, I watched
people coming to the wells for water. Almost to the minute, at
4 p.m., the first hyrax would appear, blinking in the sunlight.

Soon the glen in front of my hiding place was filled with the
little animals that spread in all directions and busily began to
feed, or drink from the deep pool in the rock crevice near by in
which water was present all the year round. Once I took them
some fruits from the *Heglig*, a large, thorny tree of the plains
that produces an edible drupe two inches long; these I scattered over the area and soon the rock rabbits were noisily
squabbling over these unexpected gifts.

Their first hunger appeased, the youngsters played, while
some of the older animals climbed the rocks overlooking the
valley, sunning themselves by stretching out at full length.
Often these individuals watched the movements in the valley
with as great a curiosity as I watched them from my rock
above. They took a continued interest in the activities of the
small human figures drawing water from the wells, and often I
would see one crane its neck or stand up to obtain a better
view of a man riding a donkey along the dusty road that
wandered through the plain below to disappear from sight
around the foot of one of the hills.

Any unusual movements excited the animals, and on one
occasion, when a wrestling match was being staged, a great
crowd of tribesmen gathered in full view of the hyraces. The
crowd and the noise attracted most of the animals of the
colony, and although the humans were several hundred feet
below them and perhaps a quarter of a mile away, the rock

rabbits lined up in their dozens to watch, seeming to enjoy every minute of the display.

There were always some individuals on sentinel duty. The glen was well hidden from the valley, but the sentries kept watch on the sky as well as over the hillsides. I always had to be careful not to make any sudden movement, for although I was well hidden on my rock as I lay full length peering through a clump of grass, I had, when I first began to observe the colony, startled a look-out on several occasions and set the whole lot scampering for cover—within less than a minute not a hyrax could be seen. After such an alarm, it was rare for them to appear again for at least half an hour.

In the open, their chief enemies were man, of course, who hunted them for their dark flesh; the cats—leopards, caracals and servals, all quite common in the hills; snakes; and a few birds of prey, the chief being buzzards, which I often saw. The hyraces seemed to recognise buzzards almost at once. Whenever one flew near, even when scarcely more than a speck in the sky, the rock rabbits vanished, but they ignored equally common falcons (such as the lanner, almost as big as a buzzard) or kestrels. Another enemy, fortunately for the hyraces never very common, was the regal Verreaux's eagle, a great black bird readily recognised by the white V of the back, and the yellow feet.

If no danger threatened, the animals became noisier and noisier, until their chattering and clucking could be heard over a wide area. The young, particularly, sometimes indulged in the maddest antics, leaping about from rock to rock, wildly running around and chasing each other in a continual game of catch-as-catch-can. Imagine a horde of the most exuberant puppies equipped with feet enabling them to run up sheer rock faces and jump with the sureness and agility of monkeys, and you have some idea of the three-dimensional play of wild hyraces.

In many areas the hyrax seems to be increasing, especially in places where its normal predators have been exterminated or severely reduced by man. Even if, as seems likely, the changing face of Africa eventually brings destruction to most of the wild mammalian population, the hyrax will doubtless survive. Like some rodents, hares, the common grey duiker and a few other mammals, its potential for survival is very great.

It possesses extra long tactile hairs distributed sparsely over its body, and these enable it to move quickly and surely through the labyrinth of heterogeneous boulders and tunnels of its home; the long hairs, acting like the whiskers of a cat, enable the animal to judge in the dark if it can pass through a space or hole, and the hairs probably also assist orientation. Thus the hyrax can run along its underground passages almost as surely and quickly as it can scamper over an open space above ground. Yet it has some enemies against which keen eyesight, agility, the nature of its habitat and gregarious habits are of little avail.

Snakes—pythons and cobras—and possibly some of the smaller carnivorous mammals—civet cats, genets and perhaps ratels—invade their subterranean home and attack them, the young in particular being vulnerable. However, even when a hyrax is trapped below ground by some enemy, it is still not defeated; it is likely to turn at bay at a narrow point, where, to prevent itself being dragged out by its pursuer, it inflates its lungs and so puffs itself up that, jammed tightly, it becomes almost impossible to extract. The intruder, faced with snapping jaws, is unable to outflank the hyrax, and few predators, even if able to pursue to this final point, could do more than withdraw gracefully under such circumstances.

The clamour of hyraces is certainly one reason why African hills are so often considered to be haunted, for the chattering, sometimes scolding, sounds they make are often interspersed with whistles and hoarse screams. One night, when I intended to sleep in the hills only a mile or so away from my house, I put down my bedroll without knowing that a hyrax colony inhabited the creviced, tumbled rocks near by. I was studying and hoping to catch a ratel that lived in a cave not far away.

Above us arose a hundred feet or so of steep, bare hillside; six or seven hundred feet below us was the valley. I had chosen this spot since the ratel's lair, which was about twenty feet below us, could be overlooked from our position through a natural cleft between two gigantic boulders. The ratel, or honey badger, was at home, we knew, and we were waiting for it to come out.

One of my men took the first watch as I settled down to sleep under a cloudless moon. Almost as soon as it was quiet, the only sounds being the distant chirp of a solitary cricket or the occasional chirr of a nightjar, I became aware of what sounded like whispering voices. As I raised my head, the voices stopped, only to start again as I put my head back on the rolled up bush-jacket I was using as a pillow. Unable to restrain my curiosity, I sat up, remaining very still, and after about ten minutes I heard the voices once more. I saw a little head poke out from the rocks on my right, scarcely six feet away; then more heads emerged from the rocks and an intense conversation began in hoarse, angry whispers — at least, that is exactly what it sounded like.

Our presence had prevented the rock rabbits from leaving their retreats, and they were not at all pleased. They chattered away to one another without ever showing themselves properly, and ground their teeth in a most ferocious manner. Their scolding must have alarmed the ratel, which did not put in an appearance; we were forced to abandon the project on that occasion, and wearily returned home about two o'clock in the morning.

As may be imagined, hyraces are seldom easy to capture alive without injury. I have caught only one adult myself which I soon released again.

Having found a small, rather isolated colony in a suitable situation, I kept the animals under observation for a few days before making any attempt to catch one. I saw that several used a particular entrance when alarmed or emerging to feed, invariably running for this hole no matter how far away they happened to be. I had a thin but strong cord net and decided to lower this in front of the entrance when the hyraces were out feeding, and then startle them so that they would rush into their warren. Of the several entrances the one I had chosen was the only one suitable for this method. Above it was a sheer, vertical face of rock about twenty feet high on top of which was a wide ledge we could approach from behind without being seen by the animals. To the right, about thirty feet away, was an ideal place to stand in concealment.

Early in the afternoon I stationed two of my men on the ledge above the entrance to the hyraces' lair; without showing themselves they could lower the net down the vertical rock to cover the hole. Standing hidden near by, I could see my men and they could see me, but the hyraces, unless they moved away from their usual territory, could not see us. The net was lowered until it was suspended a foot above the entrance, flat against the rock. It blended so well that I did not expect the rock rabbits to notice it unless it was moved and attracted their attention. I did not really expect to catch any of the little animals; I thought they would suspect something was amiss, and they were so alert and agile that I felt sure they would be too quick for us, but in the event we were lucky.

An hour or so later, the first hyraces emerged. To give them confidence, I let them feed and play undisturbed for a time. Then, at my signal, the net was lowered, fraction by fraction, until it was over the entrance. The nearest hyrax was some forty feet away. When finally the net was in position, I gave a second signal. At this one of the men disappeared from view, and about five minutes later approached the colony from the opposite direction, taking care not to conceal himself.

As soon as the first hyrax saw him coming, it gave a whistle and a grunt of alarm, and the whole colony fled for safety. Three hyraces rushed for the netted entrance, the first banging into the net, the other two close on its heels. As I dashed out of hiding towards them, one hyrax jumped up against the rock face, rebounded in a leaping somersault, and made off; the other two were mixed up with the net, but one disentangled itself before I could reach them, and climbed straight up the vertical rock face to disappear, but I was able to catch the remaining animal. It screamed with rage and fear, kicking and trying to bite, but I managed to transfer it to a sack without injury to itself or me.

Back at my house I released the captive into a prepared cage, but it was still in a very bad temper. As I tried to move it from sack to cage it bit my hand quite severely, and I had to go to bind up the wound, deep but fortunately in the fleshy part of my palm.

When I returned I was able to look at the animal properly for the first time. It was an adult male and showed no sign of forgetting its undignified treatment, facing me with fur standing on end so that the yellowish hair around the dorsal scent gland was exposed. Stamping like a rabbit with its back legs, dancing on its front feet, it rolled its eyes, and continually ground its teeth in a great effort to intimidate me.

A week later it was still as rebellious and bad-tempered as ever despite all my efforts to tame it, and as it was refusing to eat enough, I gave up my idea of putting it on exhibit in my zoo. Eight days after I had captured it, I toiled up the hillside again to the hyrax colony, and let it go. For a moment the animal stood and faced me, and then, after glaring defiance and grinding its teeth, turned and ran for home. I hope that it was able to give the rest of the colony an adequate explanation of so long an absence.

From time to time I have had adult hyraces brought in to me by hunters, but in all except two cases (both females) the animals proved intractable even after some months. Only these two adults ever became really tame and tolerated me, but they were never as friendly and dependent as the young I reared in captivity.

A hyrax* produces two young per litter, very exceptionally three, and they are born deep in the subterranean warren. According to my calculations with captive specimens, the gestation period is between seven and eight months. Although helpless at birth, it is only a few days before the well-developed and surprisingly hairy baby becomes mobile, and in two weeks or even less it may venture to the surface entrance for a first glimpse of the brightly lit world.

Like most other young mammals, immature hyraces make delightful pets. Two were born in my zoo in the Sudan, while I reared several newly born young, dug out from warrens, on a teat using diluted milk; the first few days were always difficult for the baby but I had no failures. Usually within two weeks, sometimes in a few days, an infant was able to lap milk for itself. The tiny creatures showed an almost immediate reliance in me that was touching and pathetic. Within a day or two the youngster's whole trust and affection was given, and it became very distressed if left alone, except when asleep.

One baby I had proved positively embarrassing. Nothing would satisfy Happy but to lie across the upper part of my shoe, and no offer of alternative accommodation would

* *Procavia ruficeps ebneri*, as were all the young reared.

appease him at first. For about a week I was forced to carry the hyrax about in this position and I was in great fear of treading on him inadvertently for he would tumble off twenty times a day. Fortunately at night Happy was quite content to sleep inside one of my shoes, otherwise I might have had to sleep in a chair with my shoes on.

As Happy grew he became more independent and would leave the top of my shoe to investigate, but rushed back at any alarm. I tried to attach a superstructure of bamboo and string to my shoe in order to make the little animal more comfortable and to prevent his falling off so often, but this was not very successful. When he was a bit older, however, Happy abandoned my shoe altogether and was content to trot along a few feet behind me whenever we went for a walk. He still regarded my shoes as home, however, for a long time.

I had two other young hyraces at this time, Daffy, about the same age as Happy, and Mek, a little older. They were an amusing sight when they became old enough to run about actively, all three following me around my big garden, running hard to keep up, each trundling over the ground like a furry, animated toy. They each had quite a different personality but, in common with all young hyraces, the same cry of distress. When hungry or lost they would make a continuous one-note noise, a kind of low-pitched 'brurrrr' unlike that of any other animal I have heard. This sound would continue until they were satisfied. If I stopped in the garden to allow them to catch up, and called them, Happy would always arrive first. He would rush up 'brurrrring' hard and usually pass me by; realising that he had gone wrong somewhere, he would run round and round until he fell over my foot; picking himself up, he would recognise the object of his search, and contentedly clamber on my shoe and settle down. Daffy would become very agitated at my call, but it always took him a long time to decide where I was. He would bounce around excitedly and then run about at random, falling over every obstacle. Sometimes he found me by accident, but more often he would scamper off in the wrong direction and have to be fetched. Mek, on the other hand, would plod on apparently unperturbed, continuing in a straight line that brought him to my feet. He would then 'brurrrr' to be picked up.

Mek was so-called because of his dignified bearing and regal disdain for every other animal, 'mek' being the local name for 'king'. Mek unfortunately came to a bad end because of his superior attitude, for he ignored a strange dog one day and tried to walk under its nose. That was the end of Mek, but Happy and Daffy lived a long time.

Abu Tig, a half-grown male baboon I had, used to tease many of the younger animals, although he was very wary of the snakes and larger mammals. Abu Tig was reared in captivity and knew no other life. He was very frightened of wild baboons. He was pretty spoilt, except when he had been particularly naughty, and he usually had complete freedom of the garden and most of the house, having his own sleeping box and blanket. He used to wrap himself up in his blanket, pulling it right over his head, every night no matter how warm it was. He was more or less house-trained, only excitement or fright causing him to forget himself.

Happy and Daffy were afraid of Abu Tig, avoiding him as much as possible, or running immediately to me as soon as the gawky baboon came into sight. Abu Tig's great delight, apart from attacking timid human beings, was to creep up on any unwary small animal, leap from hiding and charge, uttering his grunting war-cry. The animal invariably ran away and Abu Tig went into raptures, dancing up and down, guffawing and barking with pleasure, but he never pursued his victim far, unless it was a human.

The first time Abu Tig saw Mek, who arrived some weeks after I had adopted Happy and Daffy, he thought he had found a new dupe. Employing his usual tactics he dashed out from behind a tree as I passed, the three hyraces trotting at my heels. Happy and Daffy fled, chattering with alarm, but Mek showed no concern at all, ignoring the grimacing baboon, and continuing on his slow way. Taken aback at this indifference, Abu Tig came to a halt a few feet from Mek, stared for a moment at the hyrax, and then squatted down, pretending to play with a stick but nevertheless watching Mek who never deviated from his course, caught up with me, and cried as usual to be picked up.

Abu Tig did not see very much of Mek in the next few days because the hyrax was kept in a cage for most of the time, but whenever the baboon caught sight of him he could scarcely stop staring. His lack of success in frightening Mek seemed to encourage Abu Tig to take it out on the other hyraces, and he actually caught hold of Daffy one day and tried to bite her — Daffy was terrified but fortunately I rescued her before the baboon could do any harm. Abu Tig was becoming a problem, and I was wondering what I could do about him when the difficulty was resolved unexpectedly.

Since Abu Tig's attempt to bite Daffy, I had shut up the baboon when the hyraces were taken for their evening walk, but on this day Abu Tig had somehow become loose. Happy and Daffy were close to me, Mek some distance off, when to my surprise and alarm, I saw Abu Tig come bounding along, screaming with rage and heading straight for Mek, obviously determined to have it out with him this time. I shouted at the baboon but although Abu Tig normally heeded my voice, on this occasion he took no notice. Mek seemed quite unperturbed until Abu Tig caught hold of him and bent down to bite. There was a scuffle, but before I could reach them, Mek flew through the air as Abu Tig flung him aside and fled towards me chittering with fear, for somehow Mek had managed to bite before the baboon.

Abu Tig, who was a complete coward really, jumped into my arms and tried to hide his head — something he always did when he ran into trouble. Mek picked himself up, wandered around a little, somewhat dazed but otherwise unhurt, and then headed towards me as fast as he could run, his equanimity upset for once. When Abu Tig saw Mek approaching, he leapt out of my arms and took refuge at the top of the nearest tree, peering down through the foliage with anxious eyes as if expecting Mek to pursue him. Abu Tig left Mek severely alone after this episode and, taking no chances, he also gave up trying to frighten Happy and Daffy.

The Nuba of Kordofan, amongst whom I lived for some years, say that it was the baboon that stole the *Kako's* (hyrax's) tail. In the past, they say, the baboon had no tail and the *kako* had. One day the animals wanted to hold a dance, but there was no one to beat the drum; not one of them knew how to do this properly.

'I will go and watch the men,' said the baboon, 'and learn

how to play the drums, and then we can hold our dance.' The other animals agreed. When the baboon had found out how the drums were played, he called the other animals together again. 'I have found out how to play the drums,' he said, 'but I shall need a tail to beat them with. Who will lend me his tail?'

None of the other animals was willing to part with his tail, but in the end the *kako*, being a foolish animal, agreed to lend his tail to the baboon. The dance was held, and when it was over the *kako* asked for his tail back. But the baboon replied, 'Are you foolish, friend? I must keep the tail for ever, otherwise how shall we dance? I am not going to borrow it from you every time.'

So the baboon kept the *kako's* tail, and the *kako* was ashamed to be without a tail, and this is why he hides himself deep in the rocks, only coming out at night when the other animals cannot see him. This is also why the *kako* wails and screams, for he is crying for his lost tail.

Chapter 4

MYSTERIOUS MONSTER

I SPENT many of my spare hours exploring the pot-holes and caves in the gorge. We followed the course of the Mkulumuzi to its source in the mountains, where it was born from the reluctant seepage of moisture-saturated rocks and soil, and fed on its journey to the sea by numerous small rivulets and channels that each started in a similar manner. I also spent much time in the wilder areas of the mountains and coast, on the Sigi and Pangani Rivers, and sometimes farther afield.

Rarely I went alone, sometimes with only Kazimoto for companion, but usually I had two or three men with me. It was during these early years in Tanganyika that I first learnt something about the African bush, discovering its fascination and some of its hazards.

To me, the bush was never monotonous, never country to be passed through as quickly as possible with a sigh of relief when the journey's end was reached. Even in the miles of repetitive acacia scrub or grassland, superficially ocean-like in its sameness, there was always a variety of insects or the shock of a new experience: a flower not seen before, a curious or brilliantly coloured fruit; a glimpse of a strange rodent; the thrill of disturbing a monstrous rhino or a herd of graceful gazelle; the excitement of finding a snake; the speculation when finding a spoor or scat, the song or appearance of a bird not known, and a hundred other possibilities. There was, above all, always the feeling of freedom in the bush away from the rest of the human race and its artefacts, the tense awareness of the senses stimulated by the unknown.

Many unrelated fragments of incidents in the Mkulumuzi Gorge remain in my memory. In one pot-hole I found the recent remains of a wild pig that must have stumbled and fallen some fifty feet to the bottom, and there were bleached bones in some of the other holes. When I was crawling in the chasms, the remembrance of these discoveries conjured up visions of meeting a leopard or a lion that had survived such a

48

A crater-type ants' nest

1(c) A giant termite mound

Another type of crater-nest

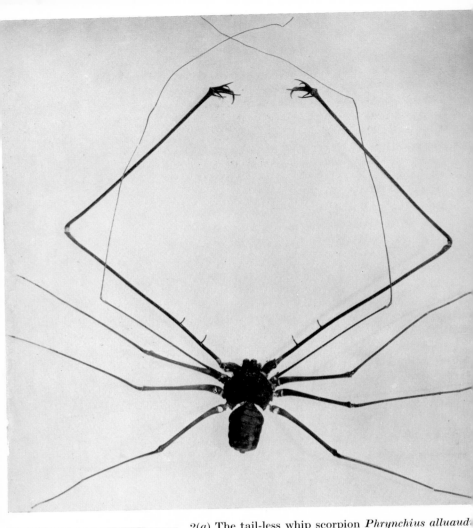

2(a) The tail-less whip scorpion *Phrynchius alluaud*

2(b) A giant longicorn beetle

fall—I never did, however. We did see leopards on several occasions in this wild area, but never in a pot-hole or cave, and once or twice we found lion-spoor. The gorge was mostly too tangled and overgrown for lion, however, whose activities were restricted to more open country although they lay up in the daytime at the cool forest edge. Even though the big cats and other large animals gave us no trouble, there were other hazards in pot-holing. I had little equipment and the thought was ever-present that when descending or ascending one of the holes the sisal rope would break, for sisal tends to fray rapidly.

I recall, too, the occasion when Kazimoto and I, armed only with two electric torches, entered a cave some considerable distance from the Mkulumuzi. The cave was isolated and the entrance hidden, but a well-defined animal track led to it, although the ground was too hard to retain prints. We found a pile of bones just around a sharp bend in the entrance passage, some of the flesh still adhering, and a sour smell of decay in the air. With one accord we turned and made our way back to the entrance, fighting a growing desire to run. Although I think the cave was occupied by hyaenas and not leopards, Jonipayo found the single pad-mark of a leopard on the compacted ground not far from the cave entrance. We left that particular cavern alone in the future.

On another day I had a near escape from serious injury when a great slab of rock, the size of a bale of hay but considerably more lethal, fell within inches of my shoulder but left me unharmed. A similar incident occurred again as we were climbing from one level to another inside a cave; a sharp, jagged piece of rock twice the size of a man's head broke away. Kazimoto, climbing just above me, deflected it with his arm, preventing it from landing on my head; his arm was severely bruised, but he was stoically indifferent to the pain, unlike the day when he had a tiny cut on his toe and yelled when I treated it with iodine.

I recollect many other incidents; my excitement, for example, at discovering large numbers of Kenya violets (*Saintpaulia*) growing with flowered profusion in and around the great cathedral-like entrance to one cave at the Amboni end of the gorge, or my delight when I found a minute, blind ant deep in one of the largest caves, a species unrecorded for more than

D

fifty years, and the Africans' incredulity that I should place any value on such an insignificant and useless *dudu*.

Altogether during that period we visited some thirty caves, thoroughly exploring nineteen of the larger ones and eight of the deeper pot-holes. Three visits I remember in some detail having recorded them in letters home.

*   *   *

The narrow entrance of the Cave of the Ants, as it became known to us, led into a passage that soon expanded allowing us to walk upright, but began to narrow again almost immediately until we were forced to bend double as floor and roof converged. We had progressed no more than about fifty paces when the silence was suddenly broken by a vast whooshing and twittering as though all the djinns in the valley had been congregating ahead of us and had now decided to leave in a hurry. Terrified bats, that seemed to be of every shape and size, poured out in an unending stream so dense that they collided with us and each other. Probably they had never been disturbed before. Atanazi, carrying the pressure-lamp, dropped it; the glass broke, the mantle shattered. In instantaneous blindness I could hear the men fleeing towards the entrance, and I retreated a few paces myself, shielding my face with my arms.

Kazimoto switched on our one electric torch. He and Felici were crouching, almost lying, on the ground, and I flattened myself against the rock face beside them. In the torch beam a thick wall of dancing bats still passed, all heading towards the cave entrance and we could do little but ward them off for the next few minutes, until at last the horde passed and only the occasional bat flew about.

Kazimoto and I examined the broken lamp.

'Go and find Atanazi and Jonipayo,' I told Felici, giving him some matches to light his way. The lamp was dented but workable; we fitted the spare mantle and glass, both surprisingly intact, working by the light of the torch. The others returned and in the bright light of the re-lit lamp we found the ground littered with bats knocked down in the wild exodus, several of them also clinging to our clothing. We spent the next few minutes removing the creatures from each other; Atanazi took one from Felici's back which promptly bit his thumb, and he let out a great screech. Until I tied the wound up with a piece of rag, the blood poured out, for these bats have razor-sharp teeth.

'Don't catch them like that,' I said, 'hold them by the wings, like this.' They were trying to catch them behind the head, either choking the bat or being bitten by it. Held by the wing tips, the bats were helpless yet unharmed. We found three kinds, two species of simple-nosed bats and a horseshoe bat.

As we moved on several more flights of bats passed, much fewer in numbers than the first panic rush, some returning to roost, and in a few moments we found ourselves standing in a great space. In this cavern, which we called Bat Hall, were more bats than I had ever imagined; every inch of the roof and most of the walls seemed to be covered with flittermice of all ages. On any jutting knob or shelf at all levels on the rough walls were females suckling their naked young. The stench was very strong. As we entered, the uproar was almost unbelievable; in spite of the previous exodus, thousands of bats remained and the air became alive once more and filled with their squeakings. Bats continually brushed our faces or banked against the light; dozens were knocked to the ground, their sonic perception unable to cope in this chaotic situation, and these began to crawl away until the ground was covered with their sprawling, awkward bodies.

With difficulty I managed to protect the lamp, and slowly, as thousands of bats left the cavern, the remainder more or less settled down again, until at last we could look about us. The cavern was about one hundred and fifty feet in length and at least forty feet high. We walked on deep, spongy, greyish bat guano, the whole in continual movement due to the hundreds of thousands of cockroaches that lived in it.

'Look around on the floor and bring me any *dudus* you find,' I instructed Atanazi and Felici, while Kazimoto and Jonipayo began to sift samples of the dry guano, looking for any insects other than cockroaches of which there were three kinds present, two cosmopolitan species and a third, common tropical kind. I wandered about with the torch. Judging by their fantastic numbers the cockroaches thrived on the rich, nitrogenous bat-dung, apparently their only food in the caves.

Our search disclosed a number of tenebrionid and carabid beetles, the former feeding on the dung, the latter carnivorous and living on other insects. Two adult histerid beetles, black, shiny and oval, occurred and we found a few larvae, probably of these adults and also predaceous, but none of these insects was very common or showed any adaptation to cavernicolous life. However, at the far end of Bat Hall I discovered a single carabid beetle with minute eyes and very elongate antennae. This little insect was obviously an habitual dweller in dark places, the long antennae enabling the almost blind beetle to find its way about. I called Kazimoto and the others over, but a prolonged search disclosed no more specimens.

In one corner I was delighted to find a minute, primitive ant (*Ponera*), slow-moving and almost blind. It was so tiny that it was almost invisible in the guano, and, although I found three workers I did not find the nest, and I could learn little about its habits. Much more apparent was a single nest of a black ant, a *Messor* species. This populous colony was nearly four hundred feet from the cave entrance and contained young of all stages. Although species of *Messor* are found over a wide area in Africa, I have seen no previous record of any kind dwelling deep in a cave and so it was an interesting discovery.

At places near the cavern walls I was puzzled to find the dismembered remains of insects arranged in small piles near fissures in the rock. Although the bats might have dropped insects occasionally, and ants often make middens of the hard, inedible parts of their prey, these little heaps did not appear to have been made by bats, ants or any of the other predators seen. I could not make out how the piles came to be there, and it was not until much later that I found they were the work of quite a different creature.

There was still enough of the day left for us to make a preliminary exploration of one or two of the several onward tunnels leading out of Bat Hall. Two we tried were only short, one being blocked by a scree-like mass that left only a very narrow gap near the roof through which it was impossible to wriggle, but the third passage looked more fruitful, the tunnel being narrow but eight or nine feet high. Leading the way with the torch, I entered, Kazimoto following with the pressure-lamp, the others behind. The walls were deeply fissured and cleft, and decorated by numerous stalactites and calcareous tufa. In places it was difficult to squeeze along the slit-like passage due to these growths. Frequently I stopped to examine the rocks or ground for specimens.

We had progressed perhaps forty yards when, looking up from examining the floor, I was startled by the shadow of an extraordinary animal, fully two feet across, sliding over a face of rock just ahead where the tunnel widened and made a right-angle turn. The huge, amorphous shape moved over the flat limestone surface to disappear from view, its distorted form moving too rapidly to be identified. Scarcely believing my eyes, and very anxious to secure the substance of such a monstrous shadow, I spun round quickly to obtain one of the collecting bags carried by Atanazi, causing Kazimoto to step back in alarm. At almost the same instant Felici screamed, and Kazimoto, surprised both by my sudden movement and Felici's shout, hit the lamp against the rock and once more we were in darkness.

Back in Bat Hall, I discovered that my assistants were all very frightened.

'What were you shouting for, Felici?' I asked him crossly.

'*Ee, Bwana! Niliona kiroja!!* I saw a monster!! It was dreadful!'

My companions were always tense and on edge in the caves, and Felici's account, vague though it was, for he could not describe what he had seen any more than I could, was enough to make them wish to escape from the caves as soon as possible. However, I put a stop to their speculations, persuaded Kazimoto to go back with me while the others agreed to stay where they were.

The lamp was quite useless, but guided by the torch with Kazimoto gripping a *panga*, we went back. Tensely we searched, but saw nothing; a noise behind startled us. Kazimoto lifted his *panga* threateningly, but the torch beam only revealed our friends, who had been so frightened on their own in the dark that they had decided not to remain behind after all. For some time we searched, and even went on down the passage, which enlarged into yet another cavern before coming to an abrupt end a little farther on, but we found nothing that resembled the 'monster' Felici and I had seen.

It was time to go, unfortunately, as it was nearly sunset and it would take over an hour to reach the car. There was no hesitation on the part of the men, who scampered back to the entrance in a very short time. As I stepped out into the welcome light after the others, Kazimoto gripped my arm. 'Look, *Bwana, chui,*' he said, pointing. Looking in the direction of his finger I saw a magnificent black leopard resting on a high rock scarcely a hundred yards away.

Although I have seen many wild leopards since, this was the finest view that I have ever had of one. Unconscious of our presence, for we had emerged unexpectedly from the cave and the sun was setting low in the sky behind us dazzling his eyes if he glanced in our direction, the leopard lay at full length on the narrow ledge of rock completely exposed to our view. The sun shone on his sleek brown-black fur through which the spots showed faintly. I studied him through my field-glasses for some minutes; he was a large animal, well over seven feet long including the lengthy tail, I judged. Like a massive carving, taking his ease on his lofty shelf, he leisurely regarded the valley where the harsh light had now given way to the soft glow of the African evening. Now and again he yawned widely, flexing the muscles of his front legs. He was probably waiting for nightfall before looking for his supper.*

We could wait no longer, although I was loath to lose the moment, for the light was fast dying. Kazimoto and the others were not disposed to linger anyway; for them, seeing the black panther was the final calamity of the day. As soon as darkness fell all the hobgoblins and ghosts would be abroad and the sooner we were back in the car the better. I walked forward slowly towards the great black cat, the men anxiously following. We were no more than thirty yards away when the animal saw us. It leapt effortlessly from its prone position on the high

---

* Melanic leopards, or panthers as black leopards are sometimes called, are rarely seen but are not uncommon in heavy rainfall areas. This was an area of moderate rainfall and black leopards were most unusual. We saw this same (?) leopard on one other occasion in the gorge where he had obviously made his home. Eighteen months later, near Voi, I saw the only other black leopard I have ever seen in the wild. Melanic leopards are only a darker variety of the common leopard, and are otherwise no different.

ledge, into a tree below, and from there silently across some rocks to disappear from view.

* * *

It was two or three months before I was able to revisit the Cave of the Ants and Bat Hall again. Atanazi never recovered from the shocks he had received on the last occasion and refused to accompany us. Jonipayo, who in his small slender frame kept a fiery spirit, was 'sick' having been involved in some sort of brawl the night before. So only Kazimoto and Felici came with me—a Felici very loath to come at all but bullied and shamed into co-operation by Kazimoto.

On this occasion we took two flashlights but left the pressure-lamp behind. When we reached the passage where previously we had seen the shadow of the strange 'monster' I told Kazimoto and a very scared Felici to search carefully. For some minutes we looked in vain. All was silent except for the noise of our slight movements, the infrequent twitter of a bat, and the loud breathing of Felici. All at once I caught a glimpse of a vague shape disappearing in a thin slit in the rock face. I shone my torch into the crevice but could see nothing in the deep fissure. The rock in this passage was full of faults, cracks and small slits or spaces between the stalagmites and the cave wall. More time passed until Felici made an incoherent noise. He was in such an imaginative state that I was not sure if he had really seen anything or not, but he swore that he had.

'Was it the creature—the monster, the *kiroja*—we saw before?' I asked. 'When we saw the shadow?'

'No, *Bwana*. This was different. More terrible-looking even. Surely a *jini*, not real, but smaller, less black, than the other thing.'

'How big?'

'Enormous,' said Felici. Kazimoto and I looked at each other.

'As big as a chicken?' I hazarded.

'No, not as big as that.'

'As big as a bat, then?'

'No. Yes. Perhaps as big, but terrible-looking. Such spirits can become any size they wish. This place is not safe,' he added with a shiver.

Making Felici move back, which he did with great alacrity, I bade Kazimoto stand on one side of the stalagmite behind which Felici said his 'monster' had hidden itself, while I stood on the other side. The stalagmite was the usual conical shape, of course, and scarcely an inch separated it at the base from the wall of the cave but near the top of the six-foot-high column there was plenty of room to insert a hand between it and the rock wall. Felici's 'terrible-looking spirit' could not be very big, however—if it existed at all apart from in his imagination.

Keeping our torches trained on the place, I carefully inserted the long, stiff leather strap of my camera case between the base of the stalagmite and the rock face. Nothing happened as Kazimoto caught the end of the strap on the other side.

'Hold your torch still, Kazimoto. Lift the strap from your side as I do. Felici, you take my torch and shine it here.' I wanted one hand free to grab anything we might flush out.

Slowly we moved the strap upwards. No result. Felici's shakes caused the torch beam to move around like a fire-fly. Shouting at him to keep the beam still, we tried again, holding the strap as tautly as possible against the rock face. This time a great spidery shape dodged out and ran rapidly along the rock into another crevice, giving me no chance of catching it. It was a giant whip scorpion.

Afterwards we kept seeing others, for this part of the cave-system was infested with them. It was the monstrous form of one of these animals, freakishly cast by the lamp on the rock face, that we had seen on our first visit; in some manner one of the beasts had moved in front of the pressure-lamp so that we had glimpsed only the greatly enlarged shadow.

Catching a whip scorpion, however, was an even more difficult matter than seeing one, for in spite of its long spindly limbs and apparent awkwardness, it could move with astonishing speed and disappear like spilt mercury. We hunted for perhaps a quarter of an hour without catching one, by which time they were very wary and remained in hiding. I tried smoking one out using dried grass, but to no avail. Nor could we poke them out with a stick. Felici, now that he was convinced the animal was real, had almost lost his fears, although he was still quite certain that the original shadowy 'monster' had been supernatural.

Eventually we gave up trying at that place, and moved along the passage carefully examining the walls. A few yards away we saw more of the creatures. This time, by careful stalking and not shining the light directly at them, I was able to catch one really big fellow and three smaller specimens with my handkerchief in about twenty minutes.

Whip scorpions are allied to spiders, and belong to the family *Tarantulidae*. The kind we found was a tail-less species, but they are all harmless as far as man is concerned despite their often horrific appearance. Our species* was a repellent-looking creature with two 'arms' (modified pedipalps) fully nine inches in length when extended in the largest specimen we caught; at the end of each of these arms were a number of long, sharp spines with one curved, hooked spine that could be articulated, closing inwards like the blade of a pen-knife, and resembling a talon. The front pair of legs were attenuated, like hairs, being in the largest specimen over a foot long. These astonishingly slender legs were used by the animal as feelers or antennae. The body resembled a spider's, the abdomen and cephalothorax together being about as large as half a crown and little thicker. The three remaining pairs of legs were also very long; each pair could span ten inches from toe to toe.

Under the circumstances, it was little wonder that Felici had been scared, for in the depth of an unknown cave, seen alive for the first time, even the real animal would be terrifying enough to many people, let alone the grotesque shadow of one, enlarged threefold, advancing over a cave wall. None of my companions had ever seen anything like it before, while I had only seen small specimens curled up in museum jars where they look harmless enough.

This was the animal responsible for the curious piles of dismembered cockroaches, beetles and other insects that I found in Bat Hall. I kept a number of these strange creatures in captivity, and the peculiar manner in which they catch their prey proved easy to study. To all intents and purposes the whip scorpion is blind, for although it possesses a battery of tiny, simple eye-spots, they are not used to help it locate or identify

* *Phrynchius alluaudi.*

its prey; only the long, deliberately-moving antennae do this. The eyes can probably hardly differentiate between total and sub-total darkness but can detect a strong light. The species I had found, scarcely recorded before, will feed on most soft-bodied insects, and in the caves its normal diet consists of some of the myriads of cockroaches, the much less common ground beetles, supplemented by other insects, such as the grass-hoppers, moths and mantids, that accidentally fly into the caves.

The long tenuous 'feelers' are held in front of the creature as it crawls slowly along; the tips of these antenna-like legs are in continual movement, slowly waving to and fro to scan the ground in front. If one of the 'feelers', in its incessant, blind searching, touches an insect it does this so delicately that the victim rarely feels anything. Despite the lightness of touch, and unalarming, sinuous movement, the prey very occa-sionally seems to sense danger and moves. If its movement is only slight, the 'antennae' follow the prey, again making con-tact. Of course, if the insect jumps or flies away, the whip scorpion loses it and has to find another victim.

The hair-thin 'antennae' are remarkably sensitive and ap-pear to be able not only to locate the prey for the 'talons' to grasp, but also to determine its size — in one dimension only. The 'antennae' will reject animals too large or too difficult for the whip scorpion to tackle, although this may be due not exclusively to size but perhaps also to texture, smell or sudden movement on the part of the quarry. For example, other whip scorpions are avoided, and I experimented with large, tough beetles, mice, worms, my own finger and inanimate things, all of which were ignored after a preliminary investigation. Of course, the 'antennae' also enable the arachnid to find its way about in the dark, to penetrate cracks and crevices of sufficient size, and to avoid those that are too small for its body.

As soon as one of the 'feelers' has contacted the prey, the other is carefully brought into play, so that the two are placed one on each side of the victim. When both 'antennae' have located the insect, the two arm-like pedipalps move slowly forward in the same deliberate manner as the 'antennae', with the spines at the end of each curved like half-clenched fingers. The 'arms' approach to within two or three millimetres, one on each side of the prey, and then make a sudden grab. If one 'claw' fails to obtain a grip, as sometimes happens, it is withdrawn but immediately extended again to regrip the now alarmed and struggling insect. When both 'claws' have obtained a good hold, the prey is moved inwards towards the jaws and eaten. As in the case of a mantid, the whip scorpion holds its victim in its 'claws' while it nibbles and gradually dismembers it, discarding the harder parts.

Whip scorpions are quite timid creatures and if the quarry shows fight, it will usually withdraw both 'claws' rapidly and retreat. I saw this happen once or twice with big grasshoppers utilising the powerful, spiny hind-legs to defend themselves, before hopping away unhurt.

Several of the caves proved to contain numbers of these whip scorpions, but they were all of the same species unfortunately. It was some years before I found other kinds in Africa.

* * *

A slight movement in the tall tangled grass attracted my attention and I ran towards it, just in time to see the tip of a snake's tail disappear. After searching for a few minutes it was Felici who found the reptile. With a shriek of '*Njoka! Njoka!*' he dropped the flattish stone he had lifted, fortunately missing the snake which had taken refuge below. The reptile was almost as startled as Felici and I was able to catch it before it was aware it was no longer hidden. Kazimoto helped me put it in the pocket of my bush-jacket, which I removed and folded carefully so that the snake had no chance of escape; we had no container large enough to hold the animal, and for once I was wearing a shirt under my bush-jacket.

The snake was one of the commonest to be found in many parts of Africa, a sun snake (*Psammophis subtaeniatus*) but at that time I had seen few, and I had not kept any alive for study. It was a fine specimen, the alternate dark and light brown stripes on the back and the pale yellowish belly with the two black pencil lines very distinct on the new skin, for it had shed the old skin only recently.

Felici came back again slowly, a huge grin on his face now that the snake was safely captive. Kazimoto glared at him. 'It would have been your fault,' he told Felici, 'if we had not caught the snake. You ran away and now you laugh.'

Felici was unrepentant, however. 'I found the snake,' he said, 'it was due to me that it was caught.'

Back in his village that night I have no doubt that Felici had an interesting tale to tell of his capture of a giant snake which he gave to the white man.

We were standing at the bottom of a cliff face on ground covered with fallen rocks some distance away from and above the river bank. It was only as we began to move off again that Kazimoto noticed the cave opening, almost entirely concealed by vegetation, including a virulent stinging nettle (*Fleurya aestuans*) that commonly occurred in many parts of the gorge. With a *panga* we hacked away the foliage, disclosing the entrance. The hole was a narrow fault in the rock face, triangular in shape, only about three feet high and no more than eighteen inches wide at the bottom. The entrance had not been disturbed by human beings for many years, if ever before, judging by the ground and vegetation. From the outside it appeared that the cave was very small, but when I squeezed through the hole, closely followed by Kazimoto and Felici, the entrance tunnel enlarged into a sizable space in which we could stand upright.

The light from our torches showed a cave the size of a small room with a high dome-like roof, and having several tunnels leading from it. As we looked round there was the usual rush of panic-stricken bats uttering their high-pitched twitter, something we were now quite accustomed to and which we ignored. I poked a stick into one deep pile of guano; it sank over four feet before touching rock.

Handing my bush-jacket, with the sun snake in the pocket, to Felici, I told him to wait while Kazimoto and I set off to investigate. Felici's nerves, never strong, were always a handicap when we were in the caves so I was glad to be able to leave him behind. He only came on these expeditions at all, I think, because of his dislike of ridicule and Kazimoto's influence over him. He settled himself on a large rock just inside the entrance, where faint light relieved the gloom of the cave.

The cave system proved to be large and complicated with three main levels each containing several large caverns interconnected by tunnels, and then a number of smaller passages at different heights again, many of which narrowed until, even by crawling on our stomachs, further progress was impossible. In the larger caverns there were well-formed stalactites and stalagmites, but in only one cave was there any falling water, a steady trickle from the roof. All the floor, even in most of the smaller tunnels, was covered with bat guano but other than the usual host of bats and cockroaches we found little life. The dung on the ground deadened all sound of our movements. The only noise was the shrill piping of the bats which, phantom-like, flew to and fro, or scuttled crab-wise across the rocks to avoid the torch beam. Although in the larger caves the roof and higher parts of the walls were covered with the creatures, almost as many as in Bat Hall, here they gave us little trouble due to the different cave levels and the numerous alternative ways of escape.

For nearly two hours Kazimoto and I mapped the cave system. We found several other openings to the outside world at the upper levels, large enough for the bats but too small for any big animal to pass. In one cavern we found a tall, mummified tree, upright still, passing through the roof into a higher tunnel. We spent a good deal of time investigating one of the lower levels where there was a slippery drop of some twenty feet which held up our progress until Kazimoto fetched a rope from the entrance. Twice we returned to find that all was well with Felici.

At last I began to reconnoitre one of the narrow tunnels some two hundred yards from where we had left Felici. I hoped that it might lead to a further system of caves, perhaps to water, for, if so, I anticipated finding some truly cavernicolous animals. Kazimoto remained at the end of this tunnel where it left a larger cavern. The passage was very like a miniature railway tunnel, with round roof and walls worn smooth by water action, but no water appeared to have been through for a long time.

The dry tunnel was just large enough for me to crawl along on my elbows when lying full length, using my feet to help push myself along, but progress was slow. It was impossible to turn round unless the space enlarged, and I would have to crawl backwards to get out again, this being much more

difficult than pushing forwards. After moving forward in this
manner for some thirty-five feet along an almost straight
tunnel, I came to a difficult bend where the passage narrowed
somewhat. Fortunately, the bat-droppings that occurred even
here made a soft surface on which to crawl, although the
nauseous and all-pervading smell of the dung and the innumerable cockroaches in the confined space made the journey
far from pleasant. Dressed only in a shirt and shorts I began to
feel chilled, for there was a great contrast between the scorching heat outside and the clammy cold inside the caves.

As I tried to negotiate the corner I could feel several cockroaches crawling inside my clothes, but there was little point in
trying to remove them for more would have taken their places.
After a struggle and several bruises, I managed to squeeze
round the bend, pushing my torch in front of me with my head.
Much to my relief the tunnel seemed to widen in front, for I
had visions of being stuck there for good, and I was just
moving forward again when my light went out.

For a second I thought that the bulb had fused, but all that
had happened was that the head of the torch had buried itself
in the guano as I had pushed it forwards. Welcome light flooded
the tunnel again as I righted the torch to disclose, to my great
consternation, a porcupine coming towards me only a few feet
away.

Which of us was the more startled was difficult to say, for it
sensed me at almost the same moment. I pushed my nose into
the guano on the ground to protect my face and lay still,
watching the animal under raised eyebrows. Although porcupines are normally retiring creatures, they are extremely
strong and have the unpleasant habit of backing towards an
enemy with their stiletto body quills raised, and the short,
stubby tail, strongly armed with much stouter but very sharp
quills, rattling rapidly to and fro. The quills are loosely
attached to the body, especially on the tail, and as the animal
may weigh over sixty pounds and measure two and a half feet
in length, it was a formidable beast to meet under such circumstances. This was my first encounter with a porcupine
outside a zoo and it was not a very helpful introduction. He
blocked the tunnel, his quills brushing the sides and roof.

For what seemed an infinite time—although probably only a

second or two passed—we faced one another, unmoving. Then, with quills rattling loudly, the porcupine half-turned and stood quivering. I lay as though dead, scarcely daring to breathe, for there seemed nothing that I could do to protect myself other than keep my head down to protect my face. Without warning, the beast stamped its feet two or three times like a rabbit, clattering its quills so loudly that I expected them to fly off in all directions, and moved backwards towards me reducing the gap between us to no more than a quill-length. If I do not do something quickly, I thought, the wretched animal is going to push those foot-long pointed quills into my head. Without further thought I roared as loudly as I could. In that restricted space it sounded awe-inspiring even to me. Kazimoto heard my bellow and told me later that he thought I had been captured by some fearful devil. It was more than enough for the porcupine, anyway. The animal set off at a smart trot down the tunnel, grating its spines on the passage wall as it went, and vanished from sight.

Kazimoto was very worried by the time I poked my dirty face out of the tunnel again. He was quite relieved to hear that I had only encountered a porcupine, not a djinn.

We started back to the entrance—I had had enough of caves for the day—but we had one more fright. Only half-way back we were halted by an ear-piercing, terror-stricken yell. Immediately another scream made us leap forward, for this time we recognised Felici's voice. Stumbling through the caves I wondered if a leopard had attacked the poor lad. As we rushed into the cavern where we had left him, he had vanished, leaving my bush-jacket lying on the ground. Kazimoto edged his way through the entrance into the bright sunlight outside to see if he had fled or been dragged from the cave. I heard a faint moan above me. Shining my torch upwards, the beam spotlighted Felici about five feet above me, clinging to some stalactites. He was apparently unhurt but badly frightened.

I helped him down and heard his story. Apparently he had nodded off to sleep in our absence; his grasp of my bush-jacket had relaxed, and it had unfolded. The sun snake in the pocket had managed to push up a corner of the buttoned flap, and had emerged. Felici was woken suddenly by the feel of something sliding over his bare arm. Enough daylight filtered through the cave entrance for him to see a three-foot-long snake in his lap, with the forepart of its body lying on his arm and its head by his elbow. With one scream of fear he had thrown away the bush-jacket and snake and, his only thought to get away, scrambled to his perch near the roof. Once there he had yelled again for good measure.

We sent the still trembling boy out of the cave, Kazimoto saying nothing, but his look was certainly eloquent. I picked up my bush-jacket. Then we searched for the sun snake, which although mildly poisonous is a very docile species virtually harmless to man. We recaptured it a few yards away where it had hidden itself in a hole but left its tail for us to see. Following Felici out into the friendly warmth of the cheerful sunshine, I brushed the bat-dung from myself, chased numerous cockroaches from my clothes, and took deep breaths of the fresh air. The dry guano came off readily, but the smell clung until I reached home and a hot bath an hour and a half later.

A puff adder

A saw-scaled viper *Echis carinatus*

A royal python *Python regius*

4(a) *Sterculia appendiculata*

4(b) Old baobab tree

4(c) Acacia tree

4(d) *Euphorbia*

Chapter 5

NOISY NEIGHBOURS

M A N Y sounds in Africa become so familiar in a short time that they form an unconscious part of the environment, as much unremarked as rumbling traffic to the Londoner or the crowing of cocks to the farmer. But the newcomer, expecting perhaps the roar of lion and trumpeting of elephant, may be surprised to be distracted by more commonplace noises — the metallic calls of tinker birds, the dirges of doves, the barking of dogs, or to-day even the din of transistor radios.

Some of the first intrusive sounds that I noticed were caused by humans, for in the dry season it is remarkable how far voices carry. Possibly the noisy habits of most unsophisticated Africans are due to the belief that he who talks softly is speaking evil or casting a spell since there is an inherent but probably unconscious fear of silence. Companionable sound drives away evil spirits and wild animals.

It was not until I went to an *ngoma*, or beer-dance, however, that I appreciated the tremendous volume of noise that human beings could produce — no political meeting, no football crowd, no parade, can compete with an *ngoma* for sheer sound, and I shall always vividly remember this first dance that took place near Muhesa one Saturday night a few months after my arrival in Tanganyika.

It was a larger gathering than usual, more important than the average village beer-festival for it followed the end of the harvest. Everybody good-humouredly gave way as Jonipayo and I shouldered our way through the shouting, laughing and already occasionally drunken Africans forming the dense crowd. Jonipayo left me under a large fig tree in the clearing where the festivities had already commenced, for he was one of the chief participants in the dancing. The drummers sat cross-legged behind their drums, the biggest drum in the centre, a smaller one on either side. Dancers, mostly men, were circling in the open space performing the curious, shuffling, arm-jerking dance common to all these occasions amongst most Bantu people. Each man or woman was entirely occupied with his or her own movements so that although they were crowded together each person seemed oblivious to anything but the rhythm of the drums.

As soon as Jonipayo arrived he was joined by two or three other star performers. Out of view, Jonipayo took off his clothes and dressed for the part. Around his waist and over one shoulder he knotted various pieces of coloured cloth. Juma, one of the other main dancers, carefully powdered Jonipayo's face with chalk dust to make it look white and ghostly, and then helped him to adjust a false beard made from goat's hair—an emblem of virility. A giant, many-stringed necklace of cowrie shells was placed round his neck, and a genet skin, complete with tail that fell to the ground between his legs, and decorated with more cowrie shells, was fastened round his loins to hang loosely like a sporran. To complete his appearance, Jonipayo put on a wig of straight hair over his own wiry thatch and fastened on his ear-rings, made from large cork stoppers 'borrowed' from my laboratory. The wig was ornamented with a few beads and several cheap watch-chains that dangled freely.

Juma was more simply dressed in tattered khaki shorts held together by little more than encrusted grime. Around his neck was tied a frayed piece of sisal string from which hung two pieces of cloth over his naked body. A further piece of cloth knotted tightly over his head gave him a piratical appearance, and his ears, too, were decorated with ear-rings of 'borrowed' corks, while in his belt he carried a horsehair switch. His most remarkable ornaments, however, were the gigantic imitation genitals suspended from his waist; these were made from cotton cloth stuffed with cotton lint.

A third dancer mimicked a woman, wearing a dress and false breasts. A fourth, with an absurd mane of sisal strands that covered his face, looked like an unclipped sealyham, and carried an immense hollow bamboo that he blew through repeatedly to make a soft but unquestionably vulgar sound.

As Jonipayo and his friends joined the dance, the tempo quickened, the women disappeared. Jonipayo was undoubtedly the star, and alone, or supported by the other main dancers, he stamped and leapt in a frenzied performance, almost every muscle of his lithe, light body in movement as he jerked and undulated to the rhythm of the drums. The flickering fire, a hurricane lamp on a pole, and the pale, placid moonlight lit the scene, and gave grey, distorted shadows to the black nimble figures, so that there seemed to be three times the number of people leaping and prancing. The noise was immense; the drums, the stamping in unison of hard, bare feet on hard, bare earth, and the shouting voices made a confused babel that could be heard a mile or more away in the still night air. Even above this pandemonium, however, rose the ear-splitting shriek of police-whistles, blown with great abandon. Now and again I could see one of the whistle-blowers prancing like a courting bird, stamping in the open space, arms flapping like the heavy wings of a rising heron, as he shrilled on the whistle with every breath. The local beer, called *pombe*, and made, in this case, from sorghum grain, was passed round in large gourds and steadily consumed, each dancer draining a huge draught whenever he stopped exhausted.

After an hour or so, I walked back through the moon-dappled trees to my car. I could bear no more, for my head was throbbing. Even after I arrived home I seemed to hear the monotonous scream of the whistles as insistent and as intermittently regular as the call of a rain bird.

On Monday I questioned a listless Jonipayo. 'Did you dance all night?'

He looked a bit sheepish. 'We danced for a long time,' he said, 'but there were intervals, and the women did not go far. We danced again near dawn.'

At the time of the *ngoma* I was living in the old rest-house on the station until my new house was built. The rest-house was a rectangular, three-roomed bungalow that should have been pulled down four years earlier but had survived in the usual fashion of 'temporary' buildings—I was the last occupier, however, and as soon as I moved the house was demolished. I was sorry for it was one of the most interesting houses I have ever lived in since various creatures shared it with me, living in the crude brick, mud-filled walls, under the thick *mkuti* (palm-leaf) thatch, and in the cracked concrete of the floor.

Almost every night, and sometimes by day, too, there would

be strange sounds from above the sagging soft-board ceiling. The pattering steps I could understand, for they could be a lizard or a rat, although I could not account for these creatures running to and fro in apparent frenzy as they did sometimes, and I was completely mystified by the occasional 'clump, clump, clump' as though some heavy-footed beast was stomping its way from one edge of the roof to the other. Several times I rushed to the trap-door in the ceiling, flashing my torch, but always too late to catch a glimpse of this heavy-weight animal. Occasionally, too, there were great bangs or thuds, and then silence. Sometimes the noises were due to bits of old cement or loose bricks dislodged by the numerous inhabitants of the roof, or to gun-like reports given out by the timbering as it expanded in the midday heat or contracted at night, but I did not feel that *all* such sounds could be explained in this manner. Alí, my houseboy, swore that the house was haunted, but if so, it was a very solid energetic ghost.

A serotine bat, lizards, insects and spiders were the main permanent lodgers of my roof. The bats made a mess of the sitting-room ceiling in places, but their faint fairy twittering was so high-pitched that it was scarcely audible. In the rains their odour pervaded the whole house although I scarcely noticed the rather sickly smell after the first few days except early in the morning before the doors and windows were opened.

Even more silent than the serotine bat were the four-inch-long, grey, semi-transparent geckoes, that congregated nightly around my lamp, as many as fifteen at a time. As soon as the lamp was lit, their ghostly forms would emerge from hiding, to flit noiselessly across the walls and ceiling to chase fluttering insects, or to lie in wait, tail twitching like that of a cat stalking a bird. Occasionally I found their white-shelled eggs, glued together in pairs, each the diameter of a silver threepenny piece, which the female rather carelessly laid in any suitable crevice and then forgot about. Apart from a rarely heard soft 'tch-tch' when feeling amorous, the only sound they ever made was when one fell with a soft plop on the floor, although this scarcely ever happened for their suckered feet gave them a sure grip on almost any surface.

In the daytime the geckoes would vanish, remaining motionless in the dark roof until nightfall. Each individual had its own hiding place to which it invariably returned. One day I caught one for closer examination, and as I held it in my hand, Ali came in. I asked him the name.

'*Mjuzi, Bwana*,' he said, giving a general name for any small lizard, as he backed away with terrified glances at the little creature lying docilely on the open palm of my hand. At that moment, the gecko, recovering from the almost cataleptic state induced by my stroking, leapt off my palm towards Ali, who fled. Most Africans regard geckoes with superstitious awe and refuse to touch them, convinced that they are deadly, the fear arising simply on account of the cryptic habits and anaemic appearance, for geckoes are amongst the most harmless creatures on earth, being about as malevolent as an earthworm. However, even a worm turns sometimes, and some twelve years later in Nyasaland I found a giant gecko (*Pachydactylus bibroni turneri*) over six inches long, with a head an inch in breadth. On first discovering this lizard at Chapananga, near Chikwawa, I chased and caught one which promptly fastened powerful jaws on my finger, hanging on like a bull terrier, leaving my finger slightly bruised and bleeding when, half a minute later, I succeeded in forcing open its jaws with my other hand.

Chasing another lizard one day, a scarlet agamid like a miniature dragon, I pursued it into the roof but it escaped. I was about to climb down when I discovered large round holes in one of the roof-joists, each hole three-quarters of an inch in diameter, and found that they were caused by the giant carpenter bees that I often saw flying round the garden visiting flowers. These bees resemble humble bees, but this kind was even larger, nearly one and a half inches long. The female is black with long white hairs, the male a rusty brown colour with wings that spanned two inches.

Some of these carpenter bees had nested also in part of a beam that jutted from the side of the house where I could watch them in comfort from a veranda chair. I studied one particular bee making her nest tunnel. She rasped away at the wood with her jaws, drilling a neat round hole, and gradually disappearing within. It took two days to complete the tunnel and then she began gathering pollen and honey on which to

feed her young. A few weeks later I sawed off the end of the
beam containing her burrow and found a tunnel eight inches
in length, the walls smoothed and polished, the end parti-
tioned into three cells, each partition made from sawdust
glued into a disc with the bee's saliva. In each cell was one
bee grub and a quantity of food, a sort of paste made from a
mixture of honey and pollen. The nest was incomplete, for
normally at least six such cells are made.

There were seven or eight other burrows in this beam, and
each female jealously guarded her own, buzzing angrily, but-
ting and clawing at any intruder—another carpenter bee, for
example, mistaking her way home, or a parasitic fly. Sometimes the deep, angry buzzing of one bee set off the others, and
then the whole beam would seem to vibrate, emitting a sound
to be heard several yards away. I observed many of these bees
over the next few years, and gradually discovered their life-
history. There was only one generation a year, and the brood
in one burrow lived together for a time, sharing the same
tunnel. Eventually, however, any male bees present were
forcibly expelled by the females; having rid themselves of the
males, the females turned on each other, until in the end only
one female was left as the sole occupier of the original tunnel.
Carpenter bees in large numbers may cause considerable
damage, and I have seen a garage roof so weakened that it
collapsed, costing the owner some £30 to repair his car.

Wagtails were a permanent part of the establishment since
they were always present around the house, and that season
two nested under the eaves.

The African pied wagtail was, I suppose, almost the first
bird that I learnt to recognise, and is one of the best-known
birds of Africa, almost invariably found wherever there are
houses. Distinctly marked black and white, with a white eye
streak, and a long tail that bobs up and down when it walks as
though suspended on a spring, this tame, cocky little bird is
very noticeable. The bouncy walk and waggling tail give it the
look of a mechanical toy and I would not have been at all surprised to see a large key jutting from one side. It was difficult
to avoid becoming intimate with them for with the slightest
encouragement they would come wandering into the house
uttering an enquiring 'chissick?' call. The pied wagtail has

little fear of man, cats or dogs, and is one of the very few birds to be tolerated by almost everybody. It is regarded as a very bad omen should the birds desert a village or fail to arrive after new huts have been built. Even the horrible small urchins, who have discovered a use for old inner tubes from which they make catapults, and spend much of their time roaming about trying to kill every bird they see, leave the pied wagtail alone.

One cock-bird became so tame that it was soon feeding out of my hand, and kept getting under my feet. He would wander in through the open door, chirping enquiringly all the time, waiting for me to give him some of the insects I used to catch for him at night. Inside the house, however, he always kept one beady eye on me, and if I made any sudden movement, he would squawk and flutter off a few feet, then walk rapidly out of the open door.

Unlike the European wagtail, the pied wagtail has a melodious, canary song that is a very cheerful sound to hear around the house. Soon after I settled in the rest-house I obtained a mongrel puppy with floppy, spaniel ears, whose delight was to chase anything that moved smaller than himself. He could never understand the wagtails; all the other birds and lizards fled from his lumbering and somewhat unsteady charge, but the wagtails, although they flew away, refused to stay away.

The first time I saw Kali, the puppy, and the wagtails was one day when Kali was resting on the lawn. A wagtail insolently walked close to him, inspected him, and chirruped within a couple of feet, causing Kali to open one eye. For a moment he stared, obviously quite overcome by this impertinence and seemingly undecided how to cope, before he leapt to his feet, barking. If the wagtail had stood its ground I think Kali would have been so taken aback that he would have subsided there and then, but the little bird simply turned its back and walked away. Kali hurled himself forward, but the wagtail, with a contemptuous chirp, flew off from under the dog's nose, perched on the roof and mocked the furious animal. Kali expended a lot of energy barking back, but gave up after a time, returned, and lay down to doze again, apparently convinced that he had done his duty and taught the wagtail a lesson that other birds, not having the temerity to come within ten yards of him on the ground, had never needed.

A few moments later, of course, the wagtails were down on the lawn again and soon one or two were strutting close to Kali once more. Kali spent most of the day seeing off the wagtails, who seemed to enjoy provoking the dog to a frenzy by flying down over his head, perching just out of reach, or parading a few yards away. By the end of the day Kali was not only completely exhausted but also quite demoralised. Thereafter he pretended that the cheeky black and white birds did not exist and they were free to come and go as they pleased.

Another habit of the wagtails was to come to one window of my house, apparently to look at their reflections. One would sometimes become furious with its image and tap beak and wings against the glass so violently that I feared it would injure itself. They also liked to walk up and down admiring themselves and chirruping at their reflections in the shiny chromium hub-caps of visitors' cars.

Although scarcely an inhabitant, the yellow-vented bulbul was another ever-present bird on or around my roof. One kind of bulbul or another is found in any garden of East and Central Africa, and my garden was no exception. This brownish, medium-sized bird is not, at first sight, very noticeable in spite of its distinctive blackish cap, the crest that can be raised and lowered at will, and the bright yellow rump below the tail, but after a short while it would be a very unobservant person who failed to remark this obtrusive bird.

Bulbuls frequently flew around my house searching mainly for spiders; I sometimes watched one flying along close to the wall, from time to time hovering with rapidly fluttering wings while it plucked a spider from its web or crevice. After swallowing the spider on some convenient perch, sometimes the bird would return to the web to remove any insect caught therein; it did not seem to mind if the insect were already dead, having been previously wrapped in a cocoon of silk by the spider. In spite of this liking for insects and spiders the bulbul is a great destroyer of fruit and can cause havoc amongst soft-fruit trees; indeed, I have seen bulbuls drunk on over-ripe, fermenting *heglig* and other fruits in the Sudan, the birds becoming more raucous than ever and scarcely able to perch without falling over.

Although the bulbul is a pleasant and persistent songster

with a wide repertoire of whistles and trills, it is a quarrelsome, noisy bird and I was often disturbed when trying to work or read in my house by their strident chattering in the garden. Besides quarrelling amongst themselves, bulbuls are always on the look out for some other animal to scold, and chatter shrilly or monotonously call 'chit, chit, chit' sometimes for half an hour at a time when a snake, large bird of prey, a cat or any other animal they regard as a danger to the community appears. Since there was frequently some animal about that they disliked, and as the bulbul is up early and one of the last birds to go to roost, it was rare for a day to pass when I did not hear their bitter scolding, often many of the other small birds in the neighbourhood joining in adding their own rude remarks.

Towards ten o'clock on many nights I used to hear the distinctive 'huar-huu' of a wood owl that had the habit of perching on the roof of the rest-house, but I did not see the bird until one day, at dusk, I heard several bulbuls making a commotion in the bushes around a large tree in the garden. I went out to investigate, and there I found a large adult wood owl motionless in a low fork of the tree, patiently waiting for nightfall to begin its hunting. One or two of the more courageous bulbuls were perched only three feet from the great owl, scolding without cessation, while others swooped down over the owl's head. I stood at a distance and watched. The owl ignored the smaller birds for a time with closed eyes, as though asleep, but in the end the persistence of the bulbuls drove it to lumbering daylight flight, and it rose followed by the triumphant mob.

The bewildered owl did not fly far but crashed into a dense thicket, and lay with wings outspread, unable or unwilling to fly farther. As I came up, however, it struggled to its feet and vanished into the thick vegetation. The bulbuls went on abusing until darkness, but the owl remained safely hidden until the indignant small birds had gone to their well-earned rest.

The bulbul is sometimes called the snake bird because its vigilant eye discovers a snake before most other birds are aware of the reptile's presence. Although I have kept no record of the number of occasions these birds have led me to a snake, it must be at least a dozen times, and sometimes I have had to search for as long as ten minutes before finding it.

I found my first vine snake in this manner. It was a Sunday

morning and I remember I was dissecting a series of sisal weevils at the time when two bulbuls began scolding. As I rose from my cane chair to go and discover the reason for the bulbuls' alarm, it collapsed under me and I fell on my back. Picking myself up I found that one chair leg had broken and sawdust was scattered over the veranda floor. The wood was honeycombed with little tunnels, the work of hundreds of tiny bamboo-borer beetles, and now I knew the cause of a tiny creaking noise that had long puzzled me — the jaws of the beetles steadily destroying my chair.

Taking the remains of the chair, which I put on the woodpile, I went to see the bulbuls which were still swearing. Searching the bushes it was some moments before I saw the vine snake, immobile, the forepart of its body jutting from a bough. The body, held so still that it was more like a branch than a living snake, resembled the greyish, mottled bark of the tree, and I nearly put my hand on it as I parted the leaves. Although I am not repelled by snakes and have an affection for many kinds, my first view of a vine snake made me hesitate before I caught it, for the reptile had a most evil look. The sinister immobility of the camouflaged body, narrow, elongate head leaf-green on top, and the expressionless eye with keyhole-shaped, horizontal pupil, made it appear especially malevolent. However, the snake moved off at that moment, rippling delicately through the branches, and fearing to lose it, I caught it by the tail. Holding it at arm's length, I carried the wriggling reptile into the house, the bulbuls following me to the door, still squawking.

I shall always be grateful to bulbuls in the Sudan for leading me to a comparatively rare little snake — the bark snake. Only about fourteen inches long, it was beautifully marked, the head darkly marbled grey, with a black, irregularly edged stripe down the back and numerous dark spots on the body. I was not quite so pleased one day when I saw several agitated bulbuls together with other small birds fluttering anxiously at the edge of a dense thicket, and I began to search the bushes, expecting to see a snake at any moment. Instead I was almost knocked over by a leopard that bounded out, and fled across the parched countryside followed by a streamer of shrieking birds. Once I had recovered from the shock, I proceeded more cautiously, hoping that cubs might be present. In the densest part of the thicket below a large tree that supported a thick canopy of climbing plants, I reached a hollowed out form, but there were no cubs, only the scratched soil where the leopard had been lying.

Perhaps the most secretive lodger in my house was a dormouse. I saw this lovely little creature only once, very late at night when I was vainly trying to finish a report. I had been quite silent for an hour or two, and I suppose that the dormouse thought the coast was clear. A faint crunching sound made me look up from my work to see a glossy grey creature with white underparts sitting on my pelmet nibbling a cockchafer. I thought it was a mouse at first, but then I saw its great bushy tail, some four inches in length, as long as its body. Startled by my movement it ran along to the end of the pelmet, leapt on to a sagging part of the plaster-board ceiling and vanished. I never saw it again. It appeared to subsist almost entirely on insects, and I was always coming across fragmentary remains of the prey around the house.

Some weeks after I moved into the rest-house, my books arrived from England, and I spent an afternoon arranging them on the bookcases, greatly pleased to have them with me at last. A few days later a very high-pitched, penetrating whine, so like the variable sound of a dentist's drill that it gave me twinges of toothache, aroused my curiosity, but look as I might I could not trace the cause. Every time I seemed to be near the sound stopped, until one day, taking a book from the shelf, I saw a handsome, inch long, metallic blue-black wasp fly out from behind the row of books. It was a sphecid or mud dauber, and this gave me a clue. Looking along the books I found its nest, firmly attached to the top of a *Textbook of Entomology*. Pulling the heavy book out I saw that the top edges of the pages were cemented together by a layer of hardened mud, and that several cells had been completed, each an inch long and as thick as my little finger.

I left the book half out of the bookcase so that I could see the top, and shortly the mud dauber reappeared through the window carrying a large blob of mud in her jaws. Undeterred by the altered position of the book she began to apply the plastic mud, crooning her ecstatic song as she swayed to and fro smoothing the surface with her jaws. After many such journeys, she finished a new cell except for one end that she left open. Next she flew back and forth bringing fourteen small spiders, one or two at a time, and stuffing their dead or paralysed bodies into the new cell. This task completed, she deposited an egg on top of the spiders, and sealed the open end with more mud.

A week later I opened one of the hard, brittle cells to find the spiders still limp and fresh, but showing no sign of life, while the tiny, fat grub that had hatched from the egg had just commenced to feed. I kept this wasp grub until it pupated three weeks later, by which time all the spiders provided had been consumed but for the skins. Ten more days passed before the cocoon opened and the wasp emerged from its prison, rested and preened awhile, before flying away, a brilliant violet-blue in the sunshine.

Mud daubers can be a great nuisance, for they build their nests, stuffed with spiders or caterpillars depending on the species, in any hidden place, the mud staining the site. Some multi-celled nests are bigger than a tennis-ball, others consist of but a single cell the size of a thumb-nail. I have found nests not only on the hidden surfaces of books, a favourite position, but at the angles of furniture, in the folds of curtains or clothes, in my typewriter, in lampshades and even, on one occasion, in an alarm clock which never worked again. The smaller mud daubers often place their single-celled nests in crevices on brick-walls or trees, but I have also found them in houses, where they favour keyholes; I even found one nesting in the top of my fountain-pen left lying for a day on my desk.

My first rainy season brought new neighbours, or at least encouraged some of the old ones to be more vocal.

Cuckoos, for example, are amongst the noisiest common birds of the continent, and one or other of the four chestnut and black coucals is to be found almost anywhere. With the rains, a pair of white-browed coucals came to nest in my garden, and their liquid bubbling call, like water being poured from a bottle, resounded lazily most of the day. Sometimes I heard them calling drowsily on a moonlit night, the resonant song being repeated only a few times and often not completed before the bird fell fast asleep again. No other cuckoo is as persistent a singer as the rain bird, however, nor do I know any bird that can be as infuriating.

The first time that I heard the rain bird, or red-chested cuckoo, was late one Sunday morning, and I thought its voice was quite pleasant mingled as it was with the calls of the water-bottle birds, the wagtails, bulbuls, shrikes, canaries, sunbirds and others in my garden. The song consists of two short and one long note repeated over and over again, and may be rendered by almost any three-syllable way you please—'do-get-up', 'it-will-rain', 'here-we-are' and so on, as one can fit a phrase to the rhythm of a train.

All that afternoon the rain bird called from a near-by *Cassia* tree. At dusk I thought 'Now it will stop', and so it did—for a quarter of an hour—before it started again and continued all through that night, most of the next day, and until two o'clock in the morning of the third day when, red-eyed and sleepless, I floundered my way through two or three hundred yards of bush to the *Cassia*, flinging handfuls of gravel until the rain bird took the hint and flew off. The next afternoon it was calling, back in the same tree again.

This red-chested cuckoo is a secretive bird, and seldom more than a glimpse is obtained as it flits away through the foliage or sings from the middle of a leafy tree. I did not see this bird in all the six days it tormented me, and it was more than three years afterwards that I had a proper view of one—a slate-grey, reddish-brown-chested bird with a barred belly and long tail, a little smaller than a European cuckoo, that flew into a tree I had climbed to study a termites' nest glued to the trunk. The cuckoo failed to notice me and almost immediately began its irritating song a few feet above my head.

Towards the end of March I spent some other disturbed nights trying to trace a new sound. I was awakened about midnight by a melodious piping. I lay half-asleep, listening. It was not a person nor yet an insect, I thought, and although bird-like in quality, no bird I knew could whistle in this manner. I fell asleep.

The next night I heard the bright little call again, almost as though in the room. Baffled and unable to sleep, I searched my room without success, and then the grasses and bushes near the house, but look as I might, I could not find the animal responsible. In the morning I asked Ali, Hamesi, the cook, and other people if they knew this sound, but they only shook their heads. Like almost all Africans, night noises were a mystery to them, being in their opinion caused by evil spirits or mythical creatures.

For several nights the whistler was absent, and then came a night of violent storm, the rain lashing the old house for half an hour until it groaned and creaked like a sailing ship, the roof leaking in a score of places. The wind and rain stopped as suddenly as it had come, and once more I heard the serenade right outside my window. I slipped out of bed, not bothering to put shoes on, and crept to the door of the bungalow, letting myself out into the warm moist air. It was pitch-black, but I dared not use my torch as I felt my way along the side of the house in case my whistling visitor took fright. Just before I turned the corner I felt something move under my bare foot. Stepping back quickly and risking a flash from my torch, I saw that I had trodden on a black snake, a burrowing viper. Fortunately I was not bitten although I must have stepped on it quite heavily for it was writhing about. These small vipers are normally seen after or during rain and rarely bite intentionally. The fangs, however, are so long that they project sometimes outside the lower jaw, and it is easy for a fang to pierce the skin.

I did not want to waste time going back into the house to find a container, so I took off my pyjama jacket, put it on the ground, picked up the reptile by its tail (the safest way to handle this snake), placed it in the middle of the coat which I tied into a knot. Leaving the burrowing viper imprisoned in my pyjama top, I went on round the corner of the bungalow.

Reaching my bedroom window without further incident, I stood there, straining to hear the piping, trying to distinguish it from the cacophony of other noises, but it had stopped. The calls of two kinds of crickets and a long-horned grasshopper predominated. I could not see any of the insects, but I recognised their songs. One, a mechanical chirp, like metal being tapped at second intervals on glass, the other cricket emitting a much faster, more insistent screech lasting for as long as thirty seconds at a time; while the long-horned grasshopper grated rustily for a second or two like an unoiled bearing. I waited, listening, until without warning the whistle came from just behind me, and shining my torch, I at last found the culprit—a tiny, white sedge frog, little more than an inch long. Undaunted by the light, the little creature puffed itself up once more and as it deflated produced a sharp, intermittent whistle —a prodigious effort that could be heard ten yards away. Then springing with one enormous bound from the window-pane to which it had been clinging with expanded, suckered feet, it was lost in the darkness.

Satisfied at last, I returned to bed, retrieving my pyjama jacket with the burrowing viper still safely inside.

It was about this time that the first toads came into my bungalow. In the dry season I had not seen a single one, but just before the rains arrived, when the horizon was filled daily with dark banks of cumulus, but the ground was still like concrete below its layer of dust, I sometimes heard the despairing, short-lived 'krark-kwaaark' from a hidden leopard or square-marked toad, impatient of the drought. As I sat reading on my veranda one evening, the first leopard toad appeared, hopping about vigorously after its long imprisonment in the earth, wet and shiny from the deluging rain outside.

The veranda light had attracted numbers of insects, the first of the great hordes that were to appear nightly during the wet weather, and soon the toad was busy walking round, expertly lapping up the fallen fliers with a flick of her gelatinous, pear-shaped tongue—a tongue attached to the front of her mouth, but free at the back so that it could be projected at will. The movement was almost too rapid to see, and sometimes the animal simply opened her mouth to grasp the prey in her jaws without using the tongue at all. She approached most insects in a kind of shambling crawl, but for any particularly succulent morsel, such as a large winged termite, she moved rapidly in ungainly hops. A big insect would be stuffed in with her hands, when she resembled a portly old party with poor table manners.

The leopard toad is a very common creature south of the Sahara. It is quite a large animal, some specimens being a full six inches long, with a warty skin, dark angular marks on the back, and a yellowish line down the vertebral column, most specimens being brown, grey-brown or yellowy-brown, but some are distinctly reddish in colour. Being found over such an enormous area, it is not surprising that it is variable in colour and markings, or that various sub-species are known.

My visitor was soon joined by others, until eight or nine toads appeared nightly for a time, arriving at sundown and staying until so gorged that their distended stomachs dragged on the ground as they walked. Although they must have discovered independently the veranda with its abundant supply of food, it was easy to imagine that the first toad told her friends, for they all appeared within three nights. Even if in the house with a corner and two doorways to negotiate before escaping, when satiated a toad followed the most direct route to the open air, despite having spent an hour or so hopping about at random in the bungalow. Each toad had a retreat to which it retired nightly, for the homing instinct is strong. When I was in the Sudan, I marked a leopard toad which came to my house for a period of more than three years. In the dry season it remained buried under a piece of old tarpaulin, to which it retired each year at the end of the rains in October. Little wonder it was ravenous when the first showers fell, and ate as many as fifty insects at a sitting, for it remained in the same spot for the six or seven dry months.

Despite its gluttony, the leopard toad takes great care not to snap up anything that might be harmful. One toad I watched carefully for several nights showed a distinct preference for soft-bodied creatures such as small moths and winged termites, but was almost as interested in many beetles and some ants. These it caught with a flick of its rosy tongue and sometimes an audible click of the jaws, the permanent smirk (which is the impression the line of the enormous mouth gives) seeming even greater as it smacked its lips after each gulp. But it would not look at common ground crickets, certain bugs, such as assassin or stink bugs, or a number of moths with unpleasant smells or oily secretions. Small mantids, grasshoppers and their ilk were devoured with relish, but the larger, more powerful species with defensive weapons in the form of spiny legs were ignored.

Some insects were so large that it was unlikely that the leopard toad realised they were edible. I saw a great stick insect, for example, so large that it straddled one small squat toad like a derrick over a crate, its body half an inch higher than the toad's head. As the stick insect jerkily moved forwards, the toad saw a fluttering moth in the distance, and hopping, upset the insect. So alarmed was the stick insect at this eruption, if such a creature scarcely more animate than a twig can be said to show alarm, that it immediately fell down, placed the legs flat against the body with antennae closed together and refused to budge for more than ten minutes.

The leopard toads seldom made much noise, however; it was very different when the male bullfrogs arrived, which they did after heavy rain had filled all the hollows with water.

These great frogs, the largest in Africa, often bigger than a saucer, were brought to life in their hundreds by the rain after their long, dry-season burial. They forgathered in the puddles, some of which were six inches deep and thirty or forty feet long, and bellowed themselves hoarse in their efforts to attract as many females as possible. Their guttural chorus drowned all other joyous calls in praise of the rain—the chirping crickets, the whistling tree frogs, the chuckling cries of the nightjars and all the medley of sounds that merged together to make up the melody of the dripping night.

Since much of the flood-water lay on the road close to the houses, the booming of the giant frogs was almost ear-shattering. As I lay in bed in the sultry darkness unable to sleep, the throbbing, gusty chorus persisted until I felt the frogs would burst, but then it ceased unexpectedly as though on a command, leaving an intensified silence for a second or two until my ears picked up the softer or more remote night noises. Then, after a few tentative croaks as a frog musician or two tuned up, the complete orchestra would start again, as obliterating as a pneumatic drill.

About midnight I decided as there was little chance of sleep I would go for a walk. It was considerably cooler outside under the lemon moon revealed at intervals by scudding clouds; a misty drizzle fell that evaporated almost before it reached the ground, rain so fine that I scarcely felt its gentle drift against my face. The light of the moon covered the ground with a glinting patchwork, the dark puddles gleaming silvery as I skirted round them. It was light enough to see breaking the smooth surface of the water the wetly-shining rows of broad

F

stubby heads that silently submerged like so many hippos as I approached, only to pop up again behind my back to reiterate their grumpy love-song. A few female frogs, smaller, more delicately built, had arrived already, each being immediately and unceremoniously grasped by a male.

Some five minutes later I found myself on a sandy roadway that ran in front of two recently built houses, as yet without gardens. In the distance I could just make out a shadowy silhouette that at first I took to be that of an animal, but I was disappointed for the next moment I saw it was human. Surprised to find anybody about at one o'clock in the morning, I stopped in the shadow of *Cassia* tree to watch. There had been a number of burglaries recently, and the antics of the figure ahead aroused my gravest suspicions. The silhouette was moving over the ground stealthily in the direction of the houses, stooping almost double, holding in its hand a stick or spear. Picking up a stout stake left behind by the builders, I walked forwards taking advantage of any shadows from cloud or tree, the frog concert drowning any slight sound I may have made.

The man, engrossed in whatever he was doing, had his back to me and was moving slowly away. As I crept up close behind him I saw it was Philip, a member of the scientific staff. Also disturbed by the frogs, he had been taking drastic but quite useless and unnecessarily cruel action, creeping about spearing all the bullfrogs he could catch. Angered at his behaviour, and yielding to temptation, I pushed him vigorously from behind so that he fell face down into a deep puddle of muddy water, and I ran. He did not see me, fortunately, and never discovered the cause of his downfall.

Chapter 6

THE INTRUDERS

IT was not until the driver ants came that I realised just how many lodgers I had in my house.

The driver, army or safari ants (*Dorylus*) of Africa are well known and much has been written of their fierce, predatory behaviour—including a good deal of nonsense, which is a pity since their habits are remarkable enough without embellishment.* In East Africa they are often called *Siafu*, the Swahili name.

The 'sausage flies', the males of these ants, have wings and large eyes and only they can fly, and in all the known species the females never possess wings, which is unusual in ants.

As in other ants, the reddish, blind worker and soldier forms are never winged but are modified females with an arrested development, incapable of reproduction. It is the workers and soldiers which do all the hunting, defend the nest, tend the young and so on, and their marching columns, sometimes consisting of tens of thousands of individuals of all sizes up to half an inch, are often seen in Africa.

Safari ants are entirely carnivorous, and have such populous colonies that they are forced to lead a nomadic life to find enough food; their 'nest' is never permanent but is more of the nature of a camping site for they rarely settle in one place for more than a few weeks. Besides the main camp site, where the great, obese female or queen and the young are found, there may be numerous very temporary clusters of ants (and some-

* Their behaviour is paralleled by the legionary ants (*Eciton*) of South America, which have similar habits. There are a number of kinds of ants belonging to the Old World family (*Dorylinae*) all of which are carnivorous, but some live in small, subterranean colonies and are seldom seen. Over fifty kinds occur in Africa, but only three or four species deserve the name driver ant and these are the most commonly observed. Even they are seen normally only after rain, on dull, cloudy days or at night, except at higher altitudes or wet places. Driver ants only bite, and cannot sting. Technically they have a sting but this is vestigial.

times young) where dumps of food may be made *en route* for the camp.

For the first year or so that I was in Tanganyika I saw only small columns of true *Siafu*, but one subterranean species* of *Dorylus* proved particularly interesting to me since it had quite an important influence on sisal weevil populations. Several times I found that the ants had invaded old sisal boles in which great numbers of the weevils were breeding, and I watched the ants carrying off any weevil larvae they could extract as well as thousands of the white oval eggs. They reduced the young weevil population of such a breeding site by as much as eighty per cent. Only larvae that were buried deeply in the tissues of the sisal bole escaped since the ants neglected no crevice they could penetrate and spent as long as an hour investigating a single bole.

The ants that invaded my bungalow in November, 1950, however, were true *Siafu*† that marched openly above ground and occurred in much more populous colonies. In later years I was to encounter the same widespread species in parts of the Congo, Kenya, Uganda, Ethiopia, Sudan, Northern Rhodesia, Mozambique and Nyasaland, although I never again found such a large colony.

Just before 5 a.m. I was awakened by Ali who seemed in a state of great excitement. The early morning was grey and cold after a wet and stormy night.

'*Siafu, Bwana!* The *Siafu* have come!' he shouted from the open door to my unresponsive ear. For some seconds I did not realise what was troubling him, but when at last he made me understand, I sent him away to make some tea while I got up, wishing to see the ants. I could scarcely see across the room in the uninviting early dawn light. Yawning and shivering in the chilly air I lowered my bare feet to the floor. Painful sensation in half a dozen places woke me up completely, and quickly I lifted my legs back on the bed. Small, reddish-brown drivers clung to my toes, some bent almost double in their efforts to drive their mandibles even further into my flesh;

---

* *Dorylus (Rhogmus) fimbriatus.*

† *Dorylus (Anomma) nigricans*, perhaps the most notorious species of tropical Africa. There are a number of races, some authorities regarding them as separate species.

others were crawling up my legs. Swiftly I picked them off and flung them on the floor. Just as I relaxed in the belief that I had removed them all, a sudden burning stab in my groin made me jump. As is usual when these ants attack there seems no end to the numbers that crawl on you within a few seconds.

There is a widespread belief in Africa that drivers do not attack until they have swarmed all over you and then, at a given signal, they all bite at once. Although there is no truth in this story it is not surprising that many people believe it.

Recently I took a friend who was visiting the country to the top of Zomba Mountain. He became quite poetic about the view as he stood looking across Domasi Valley but failed to notice the driver columns round his feet.

'You'd better move, John. There are drivers all about,' I warned him.

He looked down quickly to see the ants swarming up him, and began to try to brush them off. Of course, his movements excited the ants, which all began to bite while the others in the columns became agitated and many more swarmed up his legs.

'For goodness sake,' I said from a few yards distance, 'get away from them. It doesn't do any good to stand there hopping up and down, you'll only get more on you.'

Following my advice at last, John stumbled away, cursing aloud, carrying several hundred of the ants with him. So many were biting him now that he did not know whether to pick off those on his neck or crush those on his ankles. Driven to desperate measures, he removed his trousers as he ran, nearly falling over in doing so, and disappeared in the bushes, his shirt tail flapping. I wandered away having spotted a wingless grasshopper that I particularly wanted for the collection, and I did not see John for the next ten minutes. When he returned fully clothed, he trod as delicately as any lily-trotter until we returned to the car.

Free from immediate attack, I peered over the edge of the bed. All round the perimeter of the bedroom was a feverishly marching column of ants; my bed was surrounded on three sides, only the foot being free. Another column was hesitatingly setting out across the floor, reconnoitring every inch and making careful progress like an army patrol moving over a plain in enemy territory. Each column was at least an inch, in places nearly three inches, wide. So far the ants had made no attempt to climb on the bed, but it was only a matter of time before they penetrated every part of the room.

Hastily I dressed. As I peered down for my shoes I saw close moving files of *Siafu* crawling across one of them in an unending stream, but the other was free. I rescued it and put it on. Then, bending down again, I quickly snatched up the other shoe. The disturbed ants spread like a pool of water over the floor, running about in all directions, searching frantically for the cause of their disturbance. In that brief instant when I had seized my shoe from the floor, more than a dozen ants clung to my hand, biting savagely, a hundred more inside the shoe spreading out over the bedclothes. I fled to the sitting-room, fortunately only just invaded, one column of ants prospecting along the inside of a window-sill. Having rid myself of the remaining ants that clung to me, I made a rapid survey of the rest of the bungalow. Two foraging columns had entered by the back door, while nine other files had found their way through various windows and were rapidly advancing, keeping close to the walls.

Ali returned with the tea, treading warily, and reported *Siafu* all round the house, especially the front, but they had not reached the kitchen or his quarters. I sat on the table in the centre of the sitting-room floor, with my tea and a pair of binoculars to watch the ants, having first taken the precaution of smearing the table legs with a film of paraffin which the *Siafu*, like other ants, dislike and avoid.

The murky morning light had imperceptibly changed and a rosy opalescence made the room glow pinkly. The scurrying reddish columns had now completely encircled the room, those entering the door having joined those spreading from the windows, so that a continuous stream with various branches and tributaries flowed along, resembling runnels of blood. In the columns I noticed ants carrying prey—mostly insects of all descriptions. Apart from the numerous insects lying dazed, dead or exhausted after fluttering round the light the night before, the main captives were the cockroaches and small beetles that lived in crevices in the walls and other dark places. Although I had known there were cockroaches in the house,

I was amazed at the numbers that the *Siafu* were dragging out—they seemed infinite. Spiders came next in numbers, these probably being more numerous than most of the other creatures living in my house since they were rarely disturbed, for I liked to watch their activities.

Many of the spiders, however, escaped the ant raiders by retreating into the centres of their webs, while the squat little jumping spiders, which do not make webs, escaped by leaping out of the way. The commonest of these was banded black and white like a zebra, and spent much of its time walking stealthily about looking for insects to pounce on. If attracted by the movements of a fly or other small settled insect, the zebra spider stalked the unsuspecting creature, until a few inches away it leapt to land on the back of the fly—as big or bigger than itself—grasping it behind the head and injecting an almost instantaneous poison.

Zebra spiders are able to leap prodigiously and accurately: I have made them jump in an eighteen-inch arc by touching them with my finger, and they have even greater agility than a cat when it comes to twisting and landing in the right place.

One zebra spider at least came to grief that morning, however. I saw the spider leap away from a wandering ant only to land plumb in the middle of a marching column. It was immediately caught by the hastening ants, overpowered and dragged along with scarcely any interruption of the marching warriors.

Other spiders that do not make webs fared badly; several large tropical house spiders, brown, flattish, with long legs that sometimes spanned four inches, were dragged from hiding. These spiders lived in crevices by day and were seldom seen except at night when they come out to hunt. Most people in Africa detest them, and it is true that they look dangerous, but they are really quite harmless although courageous. I sometimes teased one by pushing my finger towards it. The spider would raise the front part of the body and spar like a boxer with its front legs, even sometimes advancing to attack as I drew my finger slowly back. They never bite unless molested, however, even if one runs over your body.

The remorseless *Siafu*, questing in every crevice and corner, carried these gangling spiders away, twenty or thirty ants to each one. I saw one spider defending itself in a hole in the wall where the plaster had come away; a crowd of *Siafu* were trying to reach it but had difficulty in maintaining their foothold on the vertical surface. For a few seconds the big spider resisted all the efforts of the ants, but soon a few of the smallest workers managed to clamber inside the hole to obtain a good grip on the arachnid, and the creature did not long survive.

By now the driver ants had established two columns across the middle of the floor, one completely encircling my table before continuing to the other side of the room. The ants of the second procession had unearthed a large solipugid, a very hairy, fast running arachnid that in Africa is often called a 'hunting spider' or sometimes a 'wind spider'. These beasts are commonest in arid regions although some kinds are found in all but the wettest regions. Some 600 kinds of *Solifugae* are known in the tropics and sub-tropics but, although spider-like, they are not true spiders: no more than is a scorpion or a mite.

The specimen the *Siafu* were carrying was a common kind in Tanganyika, about an inch and a quarter long; the ants were carrying it upside down and the strange, white mushroom organs on the hind-legs could be seen easily. These curious growths, projecting from the undersides of the legs, are flat and expanded at the ends. They are known to scientists as malleoli or racquet-organs, but, although it is easy enough to give them a name, nobody has yet discovered their purpose. Perhaps they are specialised sense-organs, but whatever they are nothing like them is found in any other known animal. The remarkable stiff hairs on the legs, some of which may be an inch long, are certainly sensory and help the animal avoid obstacles when it is rushing across the ground quickly and lightly like a piece of brown fluff blown by a strong but erratic wind. The only solid-looking parts of the soft body are the fearsome jaws; for its size this arachnid possesses jaws that few other animals can equal for massiveness and strength.

Solipugids have a very bad reputation in Africa and are greatly feared in the belief that they are deadly poisonous. Despite the terrible jaws, however, they are not dangerous to humans and have no poison apparatus. I have been bitten on two or three occasions when handling live specimens, and the bite can be quite deep and painful but it soon heals.

The *Siafu* were having considerable trouble with their captive. In the procession across the floor progress was quite rapid, but the trail then went up the wall to the window. The ants lugging the hunting spider along reached the base of the wall and attempted to drag the corpse up to the window. Close behind them were more struggling *Siafu* carrying a monstrous, furry, mygale spider — a true hunting spider, much solider and rounder than a solipugid, with a body almost two inches long. Although often seen outside these furry spiders were rare visitors indoors and I had never before seen one in my house.

Halfway between the window and floor the mass of ants carrying the solipugid fell; they all landed on the cortège of *Siafu* below supporting the mygale spider, causing great confusion. The ants scattered as if under attack, and milled about in menacing fashion as though searching for the foe. The largest soldiers stationed themselves round the perimeter of the throng, spacing themselves out and standing with threatening mandibles, head and thorax lifted almost vertically. Many of the ants seemed to consider the two unfortunate and dead arachnids to be the aggressors and piled on top of them, biting savagely. Eventually they all sorted themselves out and began once again the trek up the wall. This time they were more successful and reached the window-sill with both arachnids.

The *Siafu* trail passed through to the outside by means of a gap between the warped window and its frame, the window being closed. Ants were moving through this slit in both directions, those entering being empty-handed, those exiting usually carrying some hapless captive.

At this point other ants carrying smaller prey passed without much trouble, but the *Siafu* transporting the solipugid met a seemingly insuperable obstacle. The gap was too small. Before they found any solution to this difficulty, the body of ants carrying the mygale arrived, and it, too, was much too big. They struggled and struggled, more and more ants joining in, with dozens running all round the labourers in an erratic — almost demented — manner. In imagination I could hear them shouting advice to the ones trying to do the work.

I watched for a few minutes, but try as they might the *Siafu* could neither push nor pull their booty any further. Then, either by accident or design, they broke off a leg from the inert solipugid. Almost at once they all began to dismember the beast and triumphantly disappeared through the slit grasping the pieces.

In the meantime the ants carrying the mygale spider had retreated with their burden and were working their way across to another exit, so that the orderly flow of traffic through the gap in the window was able to continue. It was interesting to note how two different groups of ants, from the same colony, solved an almost identical problem in two different ways — one group breaking their prey into smaller pieces, the other carrying their victim away to another exit.

Another ranging column was venturing across the room from the skirting, the foremost ants tentatively feeling their way across the open floor. I was surprised once more by the cautious exploration, for I would have expected such fierce, predatory insects to be bold and impetuous at all times, especially when in such numbers. Once a route is made the ants run along without hesitation, but when a new trail is being surveyed, they seem to have no confidence, presumably because the blind warriors follow the odour left by their comrades on a well-worn path, but when trail-blazing they have no means of guidance.

I left the safety of my table, carefully jumped to a clear space on the red-polished concrete floor, and lighted a match previously dipped in paraffin. This I placed about a foot in front of the approaching vanguard. It was flaming fitfully when the *Siafu* reached it. Immediately the alarm of the leading ants spread down the column, and disorder prevailed; as usual in an emergency the ants milled about and all was confusion, and then some individuals moved forwards, reaching towards the match, trying to bite. These were singed before coming to grips, but others and still others dashed forwards until their weight actually extinguished the flame, the column re-formed, and the ants marched on over the dead bodies of their comrades.

Some of the other patrols were now exploring the *mkuti* roof, and soon began to bring back booty: a gecko, a young skink, several more spiders and a small scorpion were brought down within a few minutes. Great hordes of *Siafu* were now vanishing into the roof, attacking all the hitherto unmolested inhabitants of the considerable space there. In order to see exactly what was going on, I avoided the various roving columns, and climbed up to look through the trap in the ceiling.

Bats fluttered everywhere, squeaking—the space seemed full of them—and here and there I could see a gecko fighting for its life. I had just time to see, not more than two feet from where my head poked through the trap, a young cobra writhing and threshing about, almost invisible under a red mass of the ants, before I too was attacked.

I had been so engrossed in the chaotic scene revealed by my flashlight that I had not noticed the *Siafu* were around the edge of the trap against which my shoulders brushed. Hurriedly I jumped down, violently slapping my neck and arms where I could feel the needle jaws of the drivers digging into my flesh. On the floor I trod in more of them which swarmed up my legs, and I ran back to the security of my table. The paraffin on the legs was still sufficient, fortunately, to deter the vicious swarms that were now everywhere. I was unable to watch for the next few minutes until I had rid myself and the table of the ants. By the time I was able to take an interest again I noticed that the columns were thinner and that all the ants appeared to be leaving, most of them carrying some form of prey. It was about seven o'clock and already there was promise of a sweltering day.

Only two great clusters of ants were left; one on the far side of the room, the other slowly crossing the floor in a reddish tangled ball. The far cluster were trying to subdue a large *Typhlops*, a harmless burrowing snake common in tropical regions. The unfortunate reptile was twisting this way and that, and had discharged an unpleasant-smelling, yellowish substance from its cloacal glands (a defensive act common in many primitive reptiles) but all in vain; the *Siafu* swarmed over it in their thousands, and in a few moments the snake became limp.

At first I could not see what the second, nearer group of ants were attacking for all I could see was the seething mass of *Siafu*, but presently I saw that they also had a snake. The reptile was pinkish-brown and one I had never seen before.

I determined to prevent the ants from destroying it, for it
might be a valuable specimen. The only way was to snatch
it from the *Siafu*, although I did not relish the task. I plunged
my hand into the middle of the red mass, caught hold of the
snake, and shook it. Ants flew off in all directions but many
hundreds remained. I brushed most of them off with my other
hand, ignoring the hundreds crawling on me.

Freeing the snake took some time, for a driver is like a burr
—just touch one and it clings. I put the reptile in a screw-top
jar for safety, and then I was able to attend to myself. It took
me a very long time to find all the *Siafu* on my body, and even
longer before I was able to forget the pricking, burning pain
caused by their sickle-shaped jaws, often in the tenderest
places. Little globules of blood formed all over my skin when
I had finished, Once a driver has a good grip it is almost
impossible to force it to let go; in pulling one off the head is
often left, the mandibles still gripping as tightly as ever. In
some of the more primitive parts of Africa near the equator,
some Negroes use the *Siafu* (and other ants, but especially the
driver ants) to stitch up wounds: the edges of a wound are held
together, and the largest soldiers are caught and held to bite
so as to secure the flaps of skin together. The bodies are then
pinched off leaving the severed heads holding the previously
gaping wound closed. I have seen this myself only once when
I met a man in a remote part of southern Sudan who had a
row of dozens of dangling *Siafu* heads holding the skin together of a long, slit-like lesion in his shoulder. The wound had
healed cleanly but he seemed quite content to leave the heads
in place.

The snake, when I had time to examine it, proved to be a
centipede eater, an uncommonly found, semi-burrowing reptile. Unfortunately, although still alive, it was not worth keeping for its eyes had been eaten away, and part of the side had
been stripped of scales, in one place disclosing the vertebra. I
put it out of its misery at once.

By half-past seven the *Siafu* had all disappeared except for
the maimed stragglers or dead ones, so I was able to have
breakfast in peace. These ants only forage during the cool of
the morning or evening or night, unless the day is overcast and
damp. As soon as the sun has any power the *Siafu* vanish

underground or shelter in shady places (round the bottom of a bush, for example), often clinging together in compact balls without movements unless disturbed.

After breakfast I spent a few minutes before driving off to my laboratory examining the debris the *Siafu* had left. They had not managed to move the *Typhlops* very far, but they had partially stripped its flesh before leaving. Although the animal life in my house had been sadly reduced by the *Siafu* invasion, a considerable number of my lodgers still survived. The ants had not had time to explore everywhere on this first, brief visit, but the house had certainly proved a very profitable foraging ground, and I was quite sure they would return.

Chapter 7

THE FLIGHT OF THE Siafu

DURING the late afternoon heavy clouds lumbered over the horizon to obscure the sun, and now their black, swollen shapes drifted overhead to the accompaniment of vivid lightning flashes and grumbling thunder. As I returned home from my work a few heavy drops of rain bounced from the soil but the storm promise soon faded, the bellying clouds moving to burst like enormous black bubbles on the distant mountain slopes.

As soon as the sky clouded over, the *Siafu* had come back, at first a thin trickle, then in a flood, their methodical columns invading the kitchen and staff quarters to the dismay of Hamesi and Ali, who, with the aid of the gardener and a couple of complete strangers, retaliated by flinging earth, water and hot ashes on the ants. The *Siafu* swarmed in disorganised masses over the quarters, but fortunately the men had not disturbed the processions to the kitchen and the main house. Much to the indignation of my staff I put a stop to the mess they were making, and after some grumbling the cook went off to prepare the evening meal while I sent Ali to make the inevitable tea, leaving the ant armies triumphant.

My interest soon centred on the behaviour of the other ant colonies that had made their homes in my walls; they, too, spent their lives mainly preying on other insects, but compared with the warlike *Siafu* they were amateurs.

One column of the drivers was passing close to a hole occupied by a colony of cocktail ants (*Crematogaster tricolor*), so-called because of their habit of running along with the abdomen bent up over the back in a manner reminiscent of an earwig or rove beetle. At first, as the *Siafu* cavalcade passed by, there was not a cocktail ant in sight, although normally they marched in single file in and out of the nest all day and all night long. Chance and over-anxiety caused their downfall when a driver ant strayed out of line to the opening of their nest. The cocktail ants must have been massed just inside, and in a second the straying driver was bundled out gripped by a dozen or more excitable cocktail ants, each less than half the size of the driver, each biting and stinging in fury. At this commotion, numerous bellicose *Siafu* left the orderly column to investigate, and soon a desperate battle was in progress that rapidly turned into a rout. The cocktail ants, despite being on their home ground, having the advantage of sight and powerful stings, made little impression against the armour or immense jaws of the driver horde, and they soon fled leaving many dead on the battlefield, abandoning their young, eggs and home to the invaders. Some cocktail ants tried to save something by hastily snatching up a larva or pupa, but hampered by their burdens and running aimlessly, few escaped slaughter.

The victorious drivers re-formed and marched off carrying their spoils, but leaving behind most of the adult cocktail ants as well as their own maimed comrades.

The main concentration of *Siafu* was now in the bathroom where I stood in the bath to avoid them. Here I noticed four different colonies of a little, shiny-black ant with very long antennae, known as *Paratrechina longicornis*, and, in Swahili, in common with several other kinds of little black ants, as *Nyenyere* or *Sisimizi*. This tiny creature, scarcely longer than the width of a match-stick, is a very lively ant, has populous colonies with several queens, and often makes its home in houses.

It was soon apparent that the *Sisimizi* were more sensible than the cocktail ants which had tried to defend their nest against impossible odds, for they had fled before the invincible *Siafu* reached them, and were stationed in four separate stationary groups on the wall where they were almost inaccessible to their formidable enemies. Surrounded on all sides by a large expanse of bare wall, clustered together in four black, globular stains against the white distemper with the queens, eggs and young, each colony was in as safe a place as was possible to find in the circumstances. Being much smaller than the *Siafu*, their claws could obtain a grip on the smooth wall, whereas the *Siafu* were having great difficulty in obtaining a foothold. But the drivers are persistent, seldom defeated for long; where one way was impassable, they tried another. Now they began to climb up the corners, the edges of the door, electric light wires and curtains. Outside the house they climbed up old earthen termite tunnels, an excellent surface for them to grip.

A *Siafu* column, scaling a water pipe, soon endangered one of the *Sisimizi* colonies clustered on the wall about two feet to the left of the window. The *Siafu* reached the window frame via the pipe, causing the alarmed *Sisimizi* to move further along the wall just above my head where they again clustered, motionless. I poked the massed colony with my finger: beyond a slight disturbance the *Sisimizi* took no notice. A few ran around on the wall but very quickly returned to the main body. Their reaction to the *Siafu* seemed much more positive than their awareness of any other hazards. Like animals fleeing from a bush-fire, when insect, reptile, bird and mammal ignore all other dangers, fear of each other and of man, in face of their most ancient and terrifying enemy, so the little *Sisimizi* ignored my finger, seemingly attuned to only one peril — the *Siafu*, as ruthless a foe as any fire.

Having reached the ceiling, the *Siafu* were able to deploy down the wall which had some cracks near the top; following one of these which enabled them to retain their footing, they once again approached the *Sisimizi*, forcing them down the wall. Since the *Siafu* also marched along the bottom of the wall it seemed that the *Sisimizi* colony was doomed. By good fortune, however, I had fixed a swinging towel rail to the part of the wall the *Sisimizi* had now reached. The little black ants with their brood and queens swarmed along the smooth rail that projected at right-angles from the wall, and sheltered in the folds of a hanging towel. Reaching the rail a few seconds later, the *Siafu* did not venture along it, and the *Sisimizi* colony was saved.

When the *Siafu* all withdrew from the house an hour or so later the *Sisimizi* colony was still in the towel, remaining there all night. The *Siafu* failed to return the next day and during the morning the *Sisimizi* found their way back to their nest below the bath and settled down again.

I did not see the fate of two of the other *Sisimizi* colonies, but the fourth fared disastrously. They tried to avoid the drivers in the same manner as the others, but were driven eventually to take refuge on the open wooden window shutter

of the bathroom. A *Siafu* column followed them, drove them
to the very edge of the shutter from which there was no escape.
The *Sisimizi* were scattered, some escaped when they dropped
off to the ground, but many were destroyed and almost the
entire brood was captured.

*   *   *

Later that evening, about 8 o'clock, I was disturbed by terrified shrieks and yells from outside the house. The *Siafu* had
long disappeared from inside, having more or less depopulated
the house, but were still very numerous and active in the
grounds. I rushed outside with a torch, almost knocking into
Ali and Hamesi who arrived from the kitchen to see what all
the noise was about.

We found Koko, my pet monkey, nearly frantic with fear
and pain. Koko had a tall pole with a box at the top for him
to sleep in. Round his waist was a dog-collar, to which a light
chain was attached at night, the chain arranged to slide up and
down the pole. Koko had been sleeping peacefully when the
Siafu had soundlessly moved up his pole, and attacked, driving
him down to the ground where more of the ants swarmed in
their thousands. Now he was in a sorry state, jumping and
rolling about, chattering and screeching, covered with hundreds of biting drivers.

With great difficulty I managed to catch the monkey, release the chain, and drag him into the house where there was
light. In doing this I was once more covered with the ants, but
I had to ignore their bites to help Koko who was almost dead
with fear. There is no doubt, in spite of the comparative freedom of movement the long chain gave him, he would have
been quite dead in a short time if he had not been rescued. As
it was his shrieks of anguish subsided into little whimpers and
he appeared to lose all will to survive once in the house, for he
lay dormant. In his terror he had defecated, and the mess was
all over his coat. We took more than half an hour to remove
the *Siafu*, and after I had taken off a thousand ants I gave up
counting. Fortunately, none had attacked his eyes, although
they had entered his ears, bitten his lips, and fastened in numbers between his fingers and toes, armpits and genitals.

There is a story of an African, in an intoxicated stupor, who was put into a small shed to cool his heels. During the night the *Siafu* came and the drunken man is said to have been killed by the ants. I cannot vouch for the truth of this tale, and have never been able to obtain first-hand information of this or similar stories, but such a death is possible. A large army of these ruthless creatures, small as they are and only a minor irritation to a large animal with complete freedom of movement, could, given time, kill even a captive lion. Numbers of new-born or young mammals are killed by the *Siafu*, and any immobilised animal is liable to be attacked and destroyed.

Koko was very miserable the next day, but recovered his spirits by the day after, although for a long time he viewed with grave suspicion every small insect that came anywhere near him, leaping out of its way or shrieking.

Koko's ordeal caused me to look at the other animals that I had forgotten in the excitement of watching the *Siafu* in the house. On the veranda I had two chamaeleons, several snakes, a small monitor lizard and a crocodile that was tethered by a cord until I could find a place for it. In the morning all had been quite unharmed but I had not seen them since. At first I thought they were all still safe, but then I discovered, to my horror, that the ubiquitous *Siafu* had found them too. One of the chamaeleons, so covered by the ants that it could hardly be seen, was dead and partially stripped, its eyes eaten out. The other, in a different cage, on a higher shelf, had been attacked by only a few *Siafu*. Swiftly I removed it, pulled off the insects, and Ali took it inside on a stick to place in the bath—the only really safe place I could think of.

I next examined the snakes. Except for a young night adder they were safe for the moment. The night adder was writhing in some discomfort but had come to no serious harm. Once again I pulled off the ants, putting the reptile back in its cage in the middle of the floor where there were no *Siafu*. The monitor was unharmed, but the young crocodile had been attacked by many ants although it was still lively and far from dead. After it was freed from its tormentors it seemed little the worse except in temper.

While attending to the animals I had not been free from the attentions of the *Siafu*, and by now I had given up the attitude of a detached observer and had had enough. To Hamesi's and Ali's delight I gave them some sprayers and insecticide, and they thoroughly sprayed the veranda, destroying large numbers of the marauders. We put all the animals back to their places, and the men went off happily to spray their quarters and the outside of the house.

*   *   *

The next afternoon I set off to trace the main nest of the drivers. In spite of the insecticide the vast *Siafu* army did not seem to have been reduced at all, although now their columns by-passed my house and were foraging in my neighbour's garden some three hundred yards away.

The main roadway of the ants consisted of a shallow channel along the soil, about one and a half to four inches wide, and between a half to two inches deep. This highway extended for three hundred and forty feet with several long side roads. The number of ants was phenomenal: on the main highway alone I estimated that there were more than five hundred ants per foot of trail, and sometimes as many as a thousand, so that over two hundred thousand ants were present in the three hundred and forty feet. Some of the secondary and tertiary trails were long although carrying less traffic, and at least a million ants must have been present altogether on the ground surface at this time. It was an enormous colony, the first I had studied in detail, and probably the largest I have ever found.

Driver ant highways are magnificently constructed even though they are used only temporarily, at most for a week or two and often for only one or two days. Each path is smoothed, tunnels and causeways are made, gaps bridged, gradients engineered, and streams crossed if they are not too wide. Along the main open highway the large soldiers stood guard, spaced an inch or so apart, facing outwards with threatening jaws, and scarcely moving unless an alien insect approached. Then the soldiers would move ponderously forward and grapple with or chase off the intruder. The sentries usually chose some eminence on which to stand—a stone, clod of earth or blade of grass. No guards were to be seen, however, where the highway passed through friable earthen tunnels built by the ants at the more exposed places where the earth was soft. Where the earth was hard and devoid of vegetation, as on a man-made road, thousands clung together to make a living roof to protect the marching columns below.

Once in the Usambara Mountains I saw *Siafu* crossing a stream about two feet across, shallow but fast-flowing. They reached the edge of the stream, hundreds of the ants running up and down as more and more arrived to spread along the bank. As I watched some of the ants clung together, more and more joining them until a living chain began to extend into the water, and soon a long line of them swung out into the current. As the line lengthened the end broke away and a cluster went floating away in the current. This did not deter the others, and in due course the line of ants, about four feet long of which three feet or more floated, reached the other bank, forming a living bridge diagonally across the water. Slowly the bridge shortened until it was at right-angles to the current, and then the unending numbers on the far bank began to cross.

This is the only time I have seen the *Siafu* make a complete living bridge, and there was no doubt that it was deliberately accomplished. More often they wander along one bank until they find a complete or partially complete natural bridge, a fallen stick or reed, or grasses growing in the water, or else fail to cross the stream at all.

When flood water overtakes them, as must often happen in Africa, instead of being scattered like most ants, the *Siafu* are often found in a ball, clinging together by means of their long legs and hooked claws. Whether or not they do this of intent is difficult to answer, but the fact remains that the drivers have found a way of surviving even the heaviest flood. Entwined closely together as one mass they are light enough to float, being carried on the current until the water subsides.

I have been such globular masses several times after floods, but only once have I seen one floating in the water during a cloud-burst. On this occasion I was marooned for a while myself on a higher piece of ground made into an island by the flood. Watching the red water swirl furiously by I managed to fish out with a stick a bobbing, spinning cluster of *Siafu* that were being swept along half submerged. On dry land the ants disentangled themselves, seemingly none the worse for their ordeal, and I was surprised to find some larvae and pupae in the midst of the mass, although I was disappointed that no queen was present. I watched until the flood water had passed, but no more festoons of *Siafu* came into view.

I spent some time tracing all the trails occupied by the *Siafu* colony in my garden and the surrounding area, and I found several subsidiary 'nests' or storehouses that afternoon, where 'camps' had been established for the temporary storage of loot, and after some difficulty I traced the main nest to the base of an old *Mvule* tree (often called *Iroko*). The *Mvule* is a tall, graceful tree that may be about one hundred and sixty feet tall and some nine feet in diameter, being normally branchless for seventy or eighty feet before spreading in an elegant umbrella of leafy branches. This tree was perhaps sixty feet high and on the shadiest side the *Siafu* had thrown up a great mould of soil, varying from a foot to more than two feet high, and about five feet in diameter. Below this loose earth, deep among the roots of the *Mvule*, was the enormous brood and presumably the queen.

There was no time that afternoon to try to find the queen as the light was already failing. Before I left I noticed that a nest of the honey ant or sugar ant was situated on the other side of the tree; in spite of this the *Siafu* made no attempt to molest them. The gawky, long-legged sugar ants were running about in their stilt-legged way quite unperturbed, or perhaps unaware, of the proximity of the drivers. Yet other nests of this ant had been attacked and destroyed when the *Siafu* were out on their raids.

Wandering slowly back to the house, I spotted a nest of *Platythrea cribinodis*, a common, large, dull-black ponerine ant, a rhinoceros in the ant world for its ponderous movements and heavy armour remind one of that ungainly animal. Almost three-quarters of an inch long, these giant ants wander about singly, their formidable stings and indigestible bodies defences against almost every would-be enemy. The nest is in the soil with only a single entrance hole almost flush with the surface of the ground, without mound or crater, so that, unless the ants are moving in and out, it is rarely noticed.

The nest entrance in this case was only a few inches from

where the *Siafu* were marching on one of their main foraging trails. At their nest the great black ants were keeping a constant guard, three or four workers crammed in the entrance hole, only their heads visible. Occasionally one worker would emerge, turn round and go back in again. Although the drivers occasionally left the columns and ran over the entrance, none attacked the black monsters which ignored any passing driver. Since the big ponerine has a powerful odour (they, with others, are often called stink ants) I considered it was probably this that deterred the *Siafu* from attacking their nest. That this was not always so I discovered some years later when I watched *Siafu* destroying a nest of these ants.

Several years passed before I found out what would happen when a *Siafu* column met a column of black stink ants (*Megaponera foetens*), another common ponerine ant. These ants march in predatory columns like the *Siafu*, but here their resemblance to the *Siafu* ends since the black stink ant has a settled nest, each colony only numbering a few hundred. When foraging, the black stink ant marches three or four abreast as a rule, in close procession, perhaps one, perhaps four, yards long (depending on their numbers), and prepare no roadways. They feed almost exclusively on termites and their expeditions are extraordinarily well-organised. Scouts, having first discovered the locality of the termite nest, perhaps only a few, perhaps two or three hundred, yards away, return to the nest and shortly afterwards the army sets off, following an undeviating (but rarely the shortest) path to the termite mound. There are two sizes of workers, and on reaching the termite nest, the army disperses, each ant disappearing into the nest to emerge in a few minutes grasping in its jaws two or three struggling termites.

When all the ants are reassembled, the columns re-form and march with their prey back to the nest. The black stink ants are heavily armoured and resemble the giant ponerine ant referred to above, but are smaller. They, too, are armed with a vicious sting and smell foully if molested. The alarm in a marching army is given by an angry, scratchy sound, produced by rubbing parts of the body together, rather like the sound produced by scratching one's finger-nail rapidly on a rough cardboard surface. When one ant stridulates in this manner, all the others in the column start up, producing a noise that can be heard four or five yards away.

Both the *Siafu* and the black stink ant are very commonly seen in parts of Africa, but although I observed both frequently, the two kinds never seemed to meet. I suppose that the odds against contact between them are very high in spite of the fact that both are active only in dull or rainy weather. Then one wet day in Kenya I saw a *Siafu* column crossing a dirt road at right-angles. In those days I used to stop and examine every *Siafu* procession I discovered; on this occasion I noticed an advancing army of black stink ants heading rapidly along the road near the verge. Unless they turned aside they were bound to cross the *Siafu* highway.

I watched without disturbing either army. The hurrying force of black ants came on and eventually reached the *Siafu* procession. The *Siafu* seemed to sense their approach while the black army was still some inches away; several ran out to meet them only to turn back; the rest of the drivers kept hurrying along their path but were obviously disturbed. As the van of the black stink ants crossed the *Siafu* trail, the *Siafu* guards ran round dizzily with wide-open jaws, and the other drivers scattered over a considerable area, but none that I could see attacked the black ants. In about a minute the whole army of black ants passed without deviation through the ranks of the *Siafu*, continuing on their way in good order. The only indication they gave that they were aware of the *Siafu* was a buzzing that passed down the ranks as the leaders first met the *Siafu*, but this was short-lived.

After the passing of the black army, the *Siafu* ran aimlessly about on the road for a time, but slowly re-formed, and once more began to travel along their own highway. As with the giant solitary black ponerine, I believe the black stink ants were not attacked because of their strong odour.

A few yards from my house I noticed a strange sight. I was walking slowly along by the side of a *Siafu* trail when I saw some brown flies, about the size of a small bluebottle, hovering just above the procession of ants. I crouched down beside the *Siafu* to try and make out what was happening. One fly was resting on the soil not more than eight inches from the hurrying ants. A moment later it flew up, remained poised for a fraction of a second above the *Siafu*, and then, with beautiful precision, dropped like a hawk and caught hold of a *Siafu* larva being carried along by a worker ant, for this was not a foraging column but one where the brood was being moved from place to place. The ants were probably moving their young from a temporary camping site to the main camp.

The fly lifted the larva out of the column, gripping it with the feet, the driver ant still clinging to the other end, so that it, too, was carried into the air. A yard away the fly settled again. As the driver found a purchase on the ground, it commenced to pull at the larva, but without result. The fly maintained a hold with its front legs while standing on the other four, and there ensued a curious tug-of-war, the fly at one end, the ant at the other, with the unfortunate larva as the rope. At first, the ant, which was quite a large one, gained some ground and pulled both the larva and the fly towards the *Siafu* highway. Then the fly found good purchase for its four legs and for a moment the two insects were evenly matched. The ant then made a mistake. Letting go of the larva it rushed at the fly with gaping jaws, whereupon the fly took off again carrying the larva, settling down again some eighteen inches away to devour the grub at its leisure. The bereft ant ran round dementedly for a time, jaws still wide open, until, apparently by accident, it found itself back in the column again and hurried off making no further attempt to find its lost charge.

Several more times I saw the flies swoop hawk-like on the *Siafu* to steal larvae although they never attacked the ants themselves. In every case that I was able to observe the flies were successful. Sometimes, but rarely, a fly escaped with a larva, leaving behind the ant that had been carrying it — I could almost imagine the ant's bewilderment, for its groping antennae and haphazard movements after the theft suggested puzzled indignation. More often the fly carried off the larva with the ant still holding the other end, and a tug-of-war as I have described above would commence. If the ant let go, the fly flew off with the larva; if there was stalemate the fly would start to devour the larva even while the ant was still trying to wrest it away. Occasionally the larva broke and the fly succeeded in obtaining only part of it.

Since that day I have seen these flies on many occasions and studied others with similar habits. The commonest species belong to the genus *Bengalia* and all are alike in appearance. Not only the *Siafu* but other kinds of ants may be attacked when they are moving their nest, but I have not seen any of these flies attack the worker ants or the pupae of ants if the pupae are enclosed in cocoons and not naked.

Bengalia depressa, common in Nyasaland and Mozambique, is nocturnal and subsists mainly on winged termites. The first time I saw this fly I was collecting insects from around my veranda light in Zomba, and as I chased an unusual beetle I noticed a number of dark muscid flies, most of them settled on the veranda roof. My beetle safely bottled, I looked more closely at the flies of which there were a hundred or more. This was most unusual for muscid flies are hardly ever seen at night in Nyasaland. Standing on a chair I saw that one fly was eating a winged termite, and, as I watched, other flies were chasing the larger termites as they fluttered around the light. With so many insects bumbling and whirling about it was difficult to follow their movements, but in a moment I witnessed the actions of one particular fly.

It left the ceiling, deliberately pursued a gyrating termite, following its prey's movements almost exactly and then, in mid-air, it swooped down from just above and behind the termite and caught it with its front feet. Immediately the fly flew straight up to the ceiling again bearing the termite, settled there, and commenced to devour the prey that was almost three times as long as itself.

The horde of predatory flies each caught and ate several termites, sucking them dry. I caught a number of the flies while their attention was occupied in feeding; some of them even continued to feed when trapped in a glass tube. Holding the termite with the front feet while sucking it dry, the fly fed for several minutes before discarding the skin.

I spent over an hour watching their activities. They seemed so intent on catching their prey that nothing distracted them. I was astonished at the tenacity they showed, at their dexterity and agility; their behaviour in the air so closely resembled the breath-taking manœuvring of a kestrel that, but for the size of pursuer and pursued, and the termite's

complete unawareness of any danger, it was difficult to believe that I was watching insects and not birds.

*   *   *

At the weekend I decided to dig up the main *Siafu* camp
under the *Mvule* tree, determined to capture the queen if
possible. This was no lightly undertaken operation and would
have been almost impossible with such an enormous colony
without using insecticides.

As soon as I started to dig there was an immediate outpour-
ing of enraged ants, each ready to sink its mandibles into anything it could find. In order to give me freedom to dig with
both hands I had a man standing by armed with a pyrethrum
spray with instructions to keep the ants away from us. At first
this worked well. As the *Siafu* appeared so they were killed or
knocked-down by the insecticide, but soon the numbers became so great that my African assistant could not control
them. A group of ants reached his bare feet, swarming up his
legs, and he turned, trying to squirt himself with the spray
lance as he ran. Not looking where he was going he ran into
a tree which knocked him to the ground, spilling the insecticide all over himself. Fortunately, the chemical was only
pyrethrum which could do him no harm, but his retreat in the
face of the enemy left me undefended. I was so intent on
watching his antics that I forgot about the *Siafu*. They did
not let me forget for long. The next minute I, too, was running as fast as possible to escape the angry thousands thronging around my legs.

When later we returned to the nest, the *Siafu* covered the
ground for yards around. With the recharged sprayer we
fought our way back to the *Mvule*, and once again I started to
dig. The ground was soft on the surface but gradually became
much harder. I disclosed a root and below this found the first
cluster of *Siafu* about eight inches in diameter. Although so
many thousands had poured out to defend the colony, innumerable ants still remained in groups at the nesting site. I
eventually reached a depth of three and a half feet, excavating
altogether nine main masses of the ants, each mass consisting
of adult ants, larvae and pupae, and this depth was obviously
the limit of the camp.

The excavation took more than three hours. In one of the lowest chambers some eggs were found and I thought that the queen must be present, but a careful search failed to produce her. As the *Siafu* had been leaving, carrying their brood, for some hours previously it is probable that the queen had already left. I followed their winding trail for three hundred yards before it disappeared into dense vegetation where I lost it, for it was dark by this time and I had to watch the exodus by torchlight.

Early the next morning I looked at the camp site again, but not a single living *Siafu* was to be seen; even the dead of the day before were few, the rest having been carried off by other ants.

Since that first major encounter with driver ants, I have met them innumerable times. Even to-day I still find them fascinating to watch. Although I failed to find the queen on that first occasion, I collected my first *Siafu* queen a year later. Since then, during sixteen years, I have only collected one other myself, and been presented with two, both dead; the first queen took me more than three days to find, the second over a week. In both cases the great, almost helpless, females, which are presumably dragged along by dozens of workers when the colony is on the move, were found hidden below a great mass of workers and soldiers in holes in the ground. The female is even larger than the male, being at least four times the length of the largest soldier and many times its volume.

Although I have seen and examined so many of these ants in east, central, north and south Africa, and although some of the colonies that I have examined contained numerous other insects as 'guests', I hardly ever saw any myrecophiles marching along in the columns. I only recall one instance when I saw another insect in numbers in the columns; this was a small rove beetle, hundreds of them running with the ants.

On another occasion I found the giant male 'sausage flies' being released by the colony. This was a most odd sight. There were hundreds of the males, all trying to escape at once from a nesting site below an enormous boulder. It was after dark and I was watching the colony with the aid of a flashlight. The worker and soldier ants were trying to regulate the giant males, but had very little success. Male after male flew away, most of them attracted to my light. I noticed that some of the massive males actually flew off with one or two workers still clinging to their legs, but these let go, as far as I could see, once they were airborne. Despite the very common occurrence of male driver ants in the tropics, observations on their release from nests seem to be very rare, and altogether there is still a great deal that is not known of these mysterious creatures, savage yet disciplined, so reminiscent of barbaric man yet so different, so instinctive yet seemingly imbued with a collective intelligence, that it is probably almost as difficult for us to comprehend them fully as it is for them to understand the human race.

Chapter 8

ENIGMA

In Africa the one-eyed may be king and because I knew something about ants I was asked to go to Kenya to give advice on those associated with a mealy bug, one of the most serious pests of coffee. The ants obtain a sweet secretion from the bugs, and because they move them from plant to plant and protect them to some extent, they encourage the mealy bugs. Fortunately the ants involved were common *Pheidole*, very familiar to me, and I had a good deal of information on the nesting and foraging habits to give the research entomologists working on the mealy bug problem, and I was able to suggest possible lines of control.

On the last night of my visit I was asked out to dinner by some friends who lived not far from the Nairobi National Park. I had driven up from Tanganyika, visiting various sisal estates on the way, accompanied by Kazimoto, Atanazi and Felici.

The men wanted to see lion, about the only large animal we had not seen on our 600-mile journey. They had heard lion at night but had never seen even a picture of one so, due to the highly coloured descriptions they had had from those people in their villages who *had* seen one, they imagined a lion to be about the size of an elephant with canines like a sabre-toothed tiger. I took them with me, leaving early at 4 p.m., planning, to make a detour through the Nairobi Park before reaching my friends at about 7.30 p.m.

In case there are still people who think that a game reserve is just a large Whipsnade, I must mention that such reserves are natural regions already inhabited by wild life, where all hunting is prohibited, and no cultivations or human dwellings are permitted. A staff of Game Guards and Wardens is employed to patrol, assist visitors, prevent hunting and to keep a watch on the animals but very rarely to interfere with them. To encourage the animals to stay in such areas, for they are free to come and go, improvements are made by the provision of special trees and grasses for grazing. The only real difference

between a game reserve and other areas where animals live is
that in the game park the animals are protected and facilities
are given for humans to see them in their natural state. Most
animals quickly learn that in such regions they are protected
from man, and if food and water are adequate they do not
migrate. In those reserves, such as the Nairobi National
Park, which have motorable tracks, people are not allowed to
leave their cars and most of the bigger animals ignore the
vehicles.

The Nairobi National Park has several road entrances, but is
small as game reserves go, covering only about forty square
miles. Not long ago wild animals used to roam the streets of
Nairobi but now a long fence guards the perimeter of the Park
nearest the city. We drove in by the main gate. Travelling
around most of the circuits we saw many of the commoner
animals — zebra, Thompson's and Grant's gazelle, waterbuck,
wildebeeste, giraffe, warthogs. My men were entranced by the
giraffe particularly. Although they had heard of such beasts,
they had not really believed in their existence, but we had still
not seen lion.

I drove up through the forest, across the Kisembe River,
and to Impala Point where I had seen lion on my last visit, but
we were disappointed. Impala Point is about the highest place
in the reserve from which we could see down across the central
plain and Lion Valley to the east. I scanned the country with
my binoculars but I could see no lion or movement of game to
suggest one. This seemed our last chance, since by this time it
was about 7 p.m. and the Park closed at 7.15 p.m., so it was
time we left. In any case I was due to dinner several miles
away.

We drove away from Impala Point, then, as luck had it, I
saw a new road, one that I did not remember being there a few
months previously. Following this very recently cleared track,
expecting it to lead down to the plain again, I drove slowly for
it was rapidly growing dark and the track, unused, was rough.
After a mile or so I had to pull up for some cut branches had
been placed across our path. When I came to reverse, the
wheels spun, and the pick-up did not move.

Switching off the engine, I got out to have a look. We were
in a patch of mud. I was not worried, for all my safari kit was

still in the back and I was well equipped for dealing with such trouble.

'Atanazi, bring the hoe and dig away the mud here. Felici, you take the other one and dig here.' The soil was a particularly tenacious clay, but after a few minutes' work it looked as though the car would move, and I climbed back into the cab.

'All right,' I called, 'let's try.'

The men stepped away as I started the engine and tried to back. The wheels spun again; the men pushed. I tried forwards, but the vehicle refused to budge. Thick, tacky mud had built up under the rear mudguards, and the back of the pick-up was plastered with blotches like broken black eggs. I began to think I might be late for dinner.

After half an hour it became quite obvious that nothing short of a gang of twenty men or a tow was going to move the Chevrolet.

By now it was about 8 p.m. and quite dark. We were in one of the wildest parts of the reserve, and we did not know exactly where. I had always understood that cars were checked out of the Park at night, but apparently this does not happen —at any rate nobody seemed to be looking for us. The men were beginning to be apprehensive now that it was dark, so we all climbed into the cab to think over the situation. It was fortunate that we were all fairly thin, for the cab was built to hold only two passengers and the driver, one of my men normally riding in the open back. I hooted at intervals and flashed the lights on and off in the hope of being seen or heard, but not for long, for I did not want to exhaust the battery.

After a short time of darkness and silence while I wondered what to do, Atanazi suddenly whispered '*Angalia! Simba! Simba!*' We all sat tensed, waiting to see what the lion would do, although I could see nothing through the misted windscreen. I switched on the headlights and on the dim edge of the left-hand beam I could just make out a tawny shape in the tall grasses.

'Close your window, Kazimoto,' I said, but even as I said it the window was closed, and I was almost pushed out of the other door as Atanazi and Felici crowded towards me to get as far as possible from the side of the lion's approach. I had only the briefest glimpse of yellowish-brown before the animal

disappeared from view again, but Kazimoto, nearest the window on the other side, could still see.

'It's coming closer,' he gasped. I shoved Felici off my lap
with some irritation, pushing him back into his seat.

'There's nothing to fear,' I said. 'Just sit quiet. The lion
cannot touch you in here. It will go away soon.'

Just at that moment the 'lion' moved closer and proved to
be two Africans dressed in long fawn-coloured greatcoats. They
were two Game Scouts who had come apparently from a hut
not far away to investigate when they heard the noise of the
horn. But as the place was haunted, the night dark and full of
wild animals, and because they feared the signals might be a
trick by robbers to lure them to the place, they had crept up,
their black heads low and invisible, only the tawny coats to be
seen as they bent their way through the grasses.

'*Jambo*,' I said, 'come and help.' Kazimoto also greeted
them. Reassured that we were real and no bandits, they lent
willing hands. Even with their help, however, there was no
hope of moving the pick-up which stood as though embedded
in concrete.

'It's no good,' I said in Swahili, 'you must go to the *Bwana*
Warden and tell him to bring a lorry to pull us out.'

The game guards pretended not to understand and chattered
to each other in Kikuyu, which none of us understood.

'They must go and get help,' I told Kazimoto, switching off
the engine. He began to talk to the guards in a great gush of
Swahili. As they argued I took my torch, not very bright as
the battery was low, and examined the underneath of the car.
It was now much lower. I could just make out the top of the
differential and part of the propeller-shaft, while I could
scarcely see the tops of the springs. There was no room to dig.
The whole back and sides of the vehicle were plastered with
mud, and the muddy imprints of the hands of the five men
patterned the black paintwork, the wings and the bonnet.

The argument between Kazimoto and the Kikuyu guards
was still going on, Atanazi and Felici occasionally joining in,
but the guards knew little Swahili, only Kikuyu and a smat-
tering of English. They stood very close to the Chevrolet and
now and again looked apprehensively around.

'What do they say?' I asked Kazimoto.

'They say that they cannot leave their post to go for help as they are not allowed,' Kazimoto answered. 'I think they are afraid.'

I looked at the guards and said in English, 'You have left your post already to come to us. What are you here for? One of you could go and fetch somebody if you can't both go.'

Eventually the real reason came out. They were afraid of the animals, the ghosts and the dark. They made every excuse they could think of. The *Bwana Mkubwa's* camp was miles away. They would certainly be killed before they could reach it. There was no one there, anyway.

I became annoyed. I told them that they were both cowards, for they were well-armed with a long spear and knife each, and equipped with whistles which I suggested they blew, but they said there was nobody within miles.

'All right,' I said, 'but if you do not go this minute I will report you as soon as I see the *Bwana Mkubwa*.'

At this they reluctantly turned and started off in the right direction, but they had not gone far before they turned and began to walk rapidly back from whence they had come. I shouted after them but they only quickened their pace, so I ran and caught them up.

'That's not the way.' I took one of them by the arm. 'Come on, you and I will go together and find the *Bwana*. You,' I said, turning to the other man, 'can wait here or come with us, as you like.'

Still holding the guard by the arm, I set off with my reluctant guide. I told Kazimoto as we passed to wait by the car with the other men. I thought that if I could get the guard out of sight of the car he would then go more willingly with me, but we had only marched about a hundred yards when he suddenly twisted from my grip, and bolted. Immediately the other guard, who had been tagging on behind, also turned and ran. I was furious and gave chase after the fleeing Kikuyu, calling to them to stop, but they fled like hares through the waist-high grasses. The next moment I tripped over a small termite hill and fell flat on my face. Ruefully I rose, spat the earth out of my mouth, and, feeling foolish and angry, walked back to the car.

Kazimoto came running up. 'Are you hurt, *Bwana*?' he

H

asked. 'The *askaris* have run away; they passed us very quickly. We will not see them again.'

I was still angry with the guards and annoyed with myself for not dealing with the situation more calmly; however, the real source of my irritation was being stuck at all in the dry season in such a seemingly minor puddle. There were only two alternatives now. To remain all night squashed together in the cab or to walk and try and find help. I decided to find help.

It seemed obvious that we had only to make our way down-hill and we were bound to find the main road; once there I knew my way. Although we were disorientated at present and it was a cloudy night, I thought that once we were free from the forested region we ought to be able to see the lights of Nairobi in the distance and take our direction from them, for we were considerably higher than the city.

The men, frightened of being left alone, all insisted on coming with me. Before we left, we fortified ourselves with biscuits and I left the open tin on the driving seat.

Leading the way, I left the track to make directly across country in the direction I imagined the main gate to be. As I breasted the tall grass that grew thickly to the edge of the road I could hear the rapid breathing of the men behind me. They were even more nervous now that we had abandoned the car. Looking round I could just see their vague outlines, the taller shape of Kazimoto close to me, the squat broad figure of Atanazi whose head scarcely rose above the top of the grasses, and, bringing up the rear, the thin silhouette of Felici clutching a *panga*. It was very dark but I conserved my torch for it only produced a dim light and it was better to accustom our eyes to the night. No star was to be seen but in the east the sky was less overcast; a soft dew-like rain was falling, the drops so fine and light that I could scarcely feel them.

Gradually our eyes became used to the dark and I could just make out the close spear-heads of the grasses surrounding us as they waved in the slight breeze on their invisible stalks. Somewhere a frog gave a guttural, experimental belch, but it was not taken up by his comrades. From the trees came a loud, monotonous shrilling of 'tree crickets', which are really long-horned grasshoppers, and the ubiquitous ground crickets, which are true crickets, added their songs, but we scarcely heard such commonplace sounds, noises that were as inevitable to the African night as the darkness itself. Our ears almost ached as we listened for more ominous sounds or movements. The rustle of the grass in the mild wind simulated the sound of animals moving, and several times in the first few hundred yards I stopped to listen.

The third time I halted there was definitely something in the grass in front of us, close enough to make us all catch our breath. The dull beam of the torch showed the slow, regular movement of the grass-heads indicating the stealthy passing of the unseen animal moving at right-angles away from us. For seconds we stood still as I tried to glimpse the beast, but it was completely hidden as it unhurriedly made off. Once more we pressed on in single file. We trod through the grass for several minutes before the next alarm. Some large herbivore, gigantic in the darkness, seemed to materialise from almost under my feet, a great shadowy form that crashed away into the dark. We all stood rooted to the spot at the shock, except Felici, who fled back along the path we had trodden but the stiff grasses, pressed forward by our advance, pointed against him, and he soon fell. Calling him back we resumed our march through the tall grass and in a very few minutes we emerged on an earthen track.

I decided to turn right, although by this time none of us had much idea which direction was likely to be correct, the darkness and vegetation preventing us seeing any landmark. I looked at my watch; scarcely half an hour had passed since we left the car.

The roadway was narrow, little wider than a car's breadth, with tall trees on one side and the grassy plateau we had crossed on the other. We followed the winding track for some time without incident. The men had more or less recovered their wits now that they were out of the grass but they kept strictly to the middle of the track, casting wary glances at the looming forest on their left and the scarcely less threatening grassland on their right.

About a mile down this road, Kazimoto clutched my arm, and I stopped. Staring hard into the gloom I sensed rather than saw something moving ahead, very indistinct and shadowy, low on the ground, a slightly blacker amorphous patch almost imperceptibly changing in outline.

'Stand still,' I whispered before creeping forward a few paces and switching on my torch. The beam revealed the thick, elongate form of a snake, that by its size could only be a python, although I could not distinguish the markings from that distance. The python ignored us completely as it continued to slither deliberately over the bare earth of the track, and its head vanished in the vegetation at the roadside while its tail was still invisible at the other verge. The track was about ten feet across, so the python must have been at least twelve or thirteen feet, a respectable size even for this giant snake. I would have liked to have caught it, but much to the relief of my men, I decided that this was not the time or place. I could hardly have turned up at the main gate or Warden's Camp with a prize exhibit from the reserve, even had we been able to carry the reptile.

From that time on we heard—and occasionally saw—a variety of animals. Almost immediately on passing the place of the python, the torchlight was reflected by a number of apparently disembodied eyes; the vague forms of some largish animals resolved from the surrounding darkness but as they bolted we saw that they were nothing more alarming than zebra. The eerie, mournful cries of hyaenas, calling invisibly like distressed spirits, sometimes near, sometimes far and difficult to locate, pursued us as we crept cautiously on, and their voices did nothing to calm the fears of the negroes; for hyaenas, associated so strongly with magic and witchcraft, caused more alarm than any other animal. Atanazi started at every rustle in the bushes, and I could hear young Felici's teeth chattering behind me. Only Kazimoto kept relatively calm, although he too felt the strain. This was a most terrible thing to happen to those uneducated men; men who had been brought up to believe in witchcraft and magic, and who peopled the night with horrifying fantasies. What to me was only an interesting experience, was to them a frightful test. They were much braver than I to face the apprehensions conjured from their imagination and primitive upbringing. I had no such illusions to cope with and therefore no fear of ghosts: I knew a good deal about animals and felt no dread of them, knowing that none would be in the least likely to attack a party of men.

We walked on warily for another mile or so. To the disgust of the men I stopped to collect some termites from the small basin-shaped mounds near the roadside for they were of a kind I was unfamiliar with. We came at last to a signpost, the first we had seen. It read 'To Impala Point—Beware of Lions' in one direction, and 'To the Forest' or some similar wording in the other direction. I knew Impala Point was not far from the main road, and thus the main gate, while the forest road meandered through dense woodland and rocks for a consider-able way. There was no sign to indicate where we had come from. Naturally we voted for Impala Point, in spite of the fact that the road led uphill again while I knew that the main road must be still below us somewhere.

The men were cheered by the sight of the signpost for it was a link with civilisation. After a time, just as I was wondering if our decision had been right, the road began to descend again, and we came upon another fork that led eventually down to the plain and the main road, missing out Impala Point.

Greatly relieved, my companions were eager to push on as fast as possible, for here another notice informed us 'Beware of Buffalo and Lion' while another finger simply stated 'Nairobi'. While the Nairobi sign undoubtedly indicated the direction of the main gate, I hesitated, for the other way would take us to the Warden's Camp where there should be a lorry or a car. For all I knew there might be nobody at the gate. Then, as we stood undecided, from the direction of the Warden's Camp we heard the grunting call of a lion not far away. After this, I had no choice, and we set off towards Nairobi. The Africans were now so eager that they led the way down the broad dirt road.

We had not gone far, at the smart pace set by the men, when from behind the bushes crowding the roadside two or three seemingly enormous animals came bounding straight across the road only a few feet in front of us. The men fled back along the road. The animals, antelope of some kind, were gone in an instant. Apart from the grumbling roar of the lion, there was silence after the buck passed. Once more we set off on our seemingly endless journey. By this time we were all tired, and my companions, their energy evaporated after their fright and since we seemed as far as ever from asylum, now walked close behind me.

It was not long before there was another alarm. We heard something moving in the bush, but this animal, unlike all the others that had fled at our approach, gave us the impression that it was stalking us. When we stopped, whatever was moving invisibly on our right also stopped. As soon as we moved on again, the rustling beside and behind began again. I shone the torch, but the dim beam scarcely showed anything more than a few feet away. Again we halted to listen, but again the animal stopped. The Africans were becoming seriously afraid now, convinced that it was a lion, or worse, some fiendish beast of their imagination, tracking us. I was sure that it was just some inquisitive antelope with no other interest in us than curiosity.

Whatever it was followed us for several hundred yards, halting every time we did, but keeping pace with us as we walked. I decided the only thing to do was to counter-attack before my men were reduced to nervous wrecks.

'Stay on the road,' I whispered to them, 'and keep still. I'm going to find out what it is.'

I ran off the road and charged through the grass, swerving round bushes in my path, and making as much noise as possible, shouting loudly. Some twenty yards from the road I stopped and listened. Something was crashing away on my right. I waited a minute or two, but heard no more, so I walked back to the road, and we continued on our way. Whatever animal it had been had gone and we were no longer shadowed.

It was now after 11 p.m. and we had been walking for more than three hours. I was very footsore, for my shoes were not suitable for walking, and we were all shivering in the cold, damp air, so it was a great relief to see the main gate after another ten minutes.

At the gate there were, to our delight, some huts on the left of the road inside the reserve, and we hammered on the door of the nearest one. There was no result. We banged again without answer, and then moved to the next hut and tried that. Again nobody came. We began to think that the place was deserted. At first there was no response from the third hut we tried, but we all heard a faint movement inside. We renewed our hammering and shouting until at last we saw a light through the cracks in the wooden door, and a moment later it opened a fraction. A frightened, suspicious voice enquired who we were and what we wanted.

I made Kazimoto talk to the man. With great reluctance the *askari* opened the door a few inches wider and peered out. When he was satisfied that we were real, he came out, and, hearing his voice, more guards emerged from the other huts. They had all been frightened at our sudden appearance in the middle of the night; normally nothing would have brought them out of their huts until daybreak, and the men in the first hut had been convinced that we were ghostly robbers, trying to entice them out to kill and rob them. They were amazed and shocked to learn that we had been walking about in the reserve for some hours. According to them, on the very rare occasions when anybody had been stuck in the game park at night they had stayed in their car; it was quite irregular for us to be wandering about. The situation was beyond them.

After a good deal of talk we were reluctantly let into the gate-house where there was a telephone. Even the sergeant in charge seemed still suspicious and scarcely able to credit his senses. He told me that there was no other vehicle in the Park and that the Warden was away, but I telephoned the Warden's Camp first of all just in case he was wrong. After a long wait a sleepy African answered. The *Bwana Mkubwa* was away. No, there was no *Mzungu* (European) there; no, there was no lorry or other vehicle of any kind, and the drivers were not allowed out at night anyway. As far as he was concerned, that was that, and he hung up.

The sergeant *askari* (most of the others had gone back to bed), now convinced that our story was true, suggested that I rang a garage in Nairobi for a breakdown truck. I did so and an Indian or Goan at the other end began asking me seemingly irrelevant questions, what my name was, how I came to be where I was, what my address was, until I became impatient and told him not to waste my time if he did not want the job, but to ring off and I would find another garage. My burst of anger seemed to convince him that I genuinely wanted a breakdown lorry, and he became eager to help, so that within twenty minutes a lorry appeared at the gate. It was now after midnight.

I was not absolutely sure that I could find my car again after our long meanderings about the Park, but I knew I could guide the lorry to the general area anyway. I left my men behind. They had not the slightest intention of returning now that they had reached the security and warmth of the gatehouse. I sat in the cab with the Game Guard chosen by the sergeant as the most experienced, while the driver's mate climbed in the back.

We drove in silence for a while. It was so dark and seemed such a long way that I began to think that we would never find the car. All the Africans were convinced of it, and wanted to turn back. The Game Guard said that he had no knowledge of any new road in that part of the reserve—certainly no such road as that I described. As we drove along a narrow but well-made and travelled road, however, all at once to our left we saw in the lorry lights the glinting reflection of shiny metal; opening the window and peering out I saw that it was my Chevrolet pick-up.

There was no doubt about it, it was my car. But it was simply standing as though I had parked it in the middle of the road; there was no sign of the muddy hole in which we had left it, and the road was quite a different one. It was not a new, rough track but a well-established road. I was completely mystified. The Africans, aware of the main facts that I had told them on the way, now showed disbelief in my story of being bogged.

Leaving the lorry headlights directed on my car, we walked up to it. I could hardly believe my eyes. There was the open tin of biscuits on the driving seat just as I had left it; there were all my belongings including a camera, a ·22 rifle and other articles of value. In my haste to leave I had not given a thought about locking the car and I had left the ignition key in. The muddy handprints on the paintwork were gone and, apart from a few mud splashes around the mud-guards, the bodywork was clean.

I tried the self-starter; as usual, the engine fired almost at once, but the radiator was cold so the car had not been driven recently. It is possible, but highly unlikely, that the rain had

washed the muddy imprints from the bodywork, but the only
rain that had fallen had been so fine and misty that it was
more like a heavy dew.

I took the Game Guard, the driver and his mate round to the
back of my car and showed them the still wet mud on the
axles and springs to prove my story. I told them of other
details but, before I had finished or realised the effect I was
having on them, they fled back to the lorry and stood whispering together.

They were terrified. I questioned them. At first they refused
to tell me anything, saying that no one could talk of such
things, but, first climbing into the cab and starting the engine,
they told me something of their fears. The car had obviously
been moved, they said, and who else could have done this but
the 'little men from the woods', the *waanga*? The *waanga* were
nocturnal robbers. They could cause death by witchcraft,
and were sorcerers with cannibalistic tendencies. Who knew
whether they were really men or supernatural beings? They
were first and foremost robbers who could not resist stealing
anything, but just to talk about them could mean being be-
witched. I learnt later that there are many stories about the
waanga in this part of Kenya, probably spread by real robbers
or by the Mau-Mau.

The driver asked me what had been stolen. I looked again
while the three Africans huddled in the cab, the engine still
running, refusing to return with me to my car. I came back
and told them I could find nothing missing at all. This restored
their confidence to a small degree. The *waanga* always stole,
they assured themselves. I said that they were all talking
rubbish fit for old women; what would the *waanga* be doing in
the wilds with no habitation for miles, with nobody to rob but
dangerous wild animals?

The ways of the *waanga* could not be known by ordinary
men, they said; perhaps the little men had learnt by magic that
I was coming and had been waiting for me. Anyway, they said,
how else could I explain the facts? Perhaps, they added, the
waanga had stolen some little thing that I had not noticed;
they *always* stole.

This possibility brought back their fears. I did not argue
any more, for I could not explain the facts. I have not been

able to explain them to this day although I am quite sure there is a rational answer. There was the car, perfectly normal and ready to drive away. There was, of course, no village inside the reserve, the nearest habitation being miles away. The two *askaris*, the only known human beings within miles, who had come to my help when the car was first bogged, could not have done anything, even if the few wits they possessed had not been frightened out of them much earlier on. I was quite sure that they had gone back to their hut, wherever it was, and slammed the door. There was not a car, lorry or other vehicle in the reserve. It would have taken some twenty men to have lifted the car, and even if the men had been there one of them would have had to be a driver, and either they would have waited for a reward or stolen something. The tin of biscuits on the driving seat had not been moved, apparently, and without moving it no one could have driven the car. It could not have been an animal, an elephant or rhino for example, that moved the car, for there were no marks, no spoor, and the vehicle had obviously been driven or pushed along the road in a straight line. Such a possibility was inconceivable, anyway. In fact, there appeared to be no logical answer.

The lorry men and the *askari* would not wait another minute in that place. I had not even time to walk back to my car again before they turned the lorry and drove quickly away.

The lorry lights faded in the distance and I was alone. The hyaenas were still calling but otherwise all was still after the clatter of the lorry. I was very tired, but I could not leave without some attempt to explain the mystery. Taking my torch I walked back along the road behind my car. I saw only a well-used roadway with numerous wheel-tracks, and no sign of the muddy patch I was looking for. There was no muddy track from my vehicle on the road, and no dollops of mud as I would have expected. My weariness overcame me, my torch was about spent, so when I was about a hundred yards away from the car I turned back.

In the car I drove for a short distance, perhaps a quarter of a mile, back along the road but I found no trace of the scene of our mishap. I did not want anything else to happen, so I turned about and drove back to the main gate, determined to return the next day to look in daylight. Unfortunately, however, I was unable to do this for, after my adventures, I over-slept and had only just time to reach Moshi where I was due to meet various people in the afternoon. It was not for six years that I had the opportunity to re-visit the Nairobi National Park when searching the whole area for the road on which I became bogged six years before, I could find no track remotely like it.

Chapter 9

THE SILENT ONES

NOBODY at all seems to have any sympathy for crocodiles. While there are people who will defend almost any other animal, this unfortunate reptile seems to be beyond the pale. Ruthlessly poisoned, shot, blown-up, hooked, speared and trapped, it is little wonder that crocodiles become rarer with each year that passes and have disappeared from many regions where they were previously common.

All the same, the crocodile is not yet in much danger of extinction. Poisoning is out of favour in most areas due to the hazard to fish or other livestock, and because poisoned crocodiles are rarely recovered before the skin has deteriorated and is of little commercial use. The favourite way of shooting crocodiles — and the most successful — is to hunt them at night with a powerful light when they can be approached closely, their eyes reflecting the light thus making an easy target. The rewards of crocodile-hunting are not large, and few men are willing or able to take up such an arduous life; those that do rarely continue for long. The only skins worth obtaining are those from the bellies of large crocodiles; the licensed hunter, therefore, works the area allocated to him by the government, killing as many mature crocodiles as he can find, but ignoring the younger specimens, which, after he has gone, may be left in peace for years. When unmolested by man, crocodiles often increase rapidly, and still probably account for more human deaths on the continent than any other kind of wild beast.

Crocodiles in their natural state are normally very timid animals in spite of their formidable size, strength, armour and teeth, and are loath to be seen, attacking from concealment of dense reeds or from below the water surface. But even such a primitive animal is not always predictable. Thus crocodiles occasionally become bolder in remote areas where people have little means of killing them, and may become man-eaters, even attacking people on sight without much effort at concealment. Despite many stories of such beasts, however, they must be rare. Of course, given the right conditions any crocodile about six feet in length or over is liable to attack a human being, probably making no distinction between a woman drawing water and a bushbuck coming to drink.

It is curious how in some localities crocodiles more or less ignore people, while elsewhere they are known as man-eaters. Nobody seems to have offered any adequate explanation of this. One river I knew in Tanganyika was full of crocodiles, and the villagers drew the muddy water at a point that seemed ideal for attack, but they assured me that they were never bothered by the reptiles, and certainly nobody seemed to worry. They drew water, swam and bathed apparently without a thought for some quite large crocs only a short way away. Yet, on that same river, further downstream, other villagers would not venture in the water, or draw water except by employing a gourd on the end of a long pole.

How much the above sort of evidence is to be relied upon is difficult to say, for primitive Africans, like uneducated people the world over, often have very weird ideas concerning animals. I was told that one river ford was quite safe, although the water was often nearly chest deep, and Africans used it continually despite the crocodiles. But some time later a woman was caught and dragged off by a crocodile in full view of half a dozen people. Thereafter this ford had a very bad name and was not used for a while, but such is the fatalism of the negro concerning death from wild animals, that soon people were using the ford again heedless of the danger, no attempt being made to kill or drive the crocodiles away. In any case the local witch-doctor, not the crocodile, received all the blame for the woman's death.

Many Africans believe in were-crocodiles, and often deaths caused by the reptiles are thought to have been caused by some human enemy, who, at will, was able to transform himself into a crocodile. In the past, many unfortunate people, supposed to possess this ability, have been done to death, and even to-day people suspected of such witchcraft may be killed or ostracised. Only a year or two ago I saw an account in an Arabic newspaper of a crocodile-man in Dongola, and recently, two and a half thousand miles south of Dongola, there came to light another case in a primitive region of Nyasaland I know well, where the supposed power of men to turn into crocodiles is accepted readily.

A man was worried because his granddaughter was be-witched, and decided that she must die. So he went to a sorcerer who could turn himself into a crocodile. When the crocodile-man demanded a fee of £2 for the murder of the girl, the grandfather paid him half on account, promising to give him the other £1 after the murder.

The were-crocodile carried out the crime, and all thought or pretended to think, the girl had been killed by a crocodile, but the grandfather, deciding that £1 was enough, would not pay the rest. The crocodile-man, justly incensed, and possibly finding his spells had no effect on the grandfather, took the matter to the local court, summonsing the grandfather for debt.

Of course the reason for the debt had to be given, and the indignant crocodile-man, in his innocence, and only concerned that he had been defrauded, told the court of the circumstances. Both men were convicted of murder.

Such cases rarely reach the ears of authority, for few Africans these days are so innocent as to believe the peculiar justice imposed by an alien world will tolerate murder in any form, even when the murderer is a powerful wizard who threatens the court with his magic. However, many such murders take place every year and sometimes a man claiming to be a were-crocodile (or were-leopard, were-hyaena or other animal) will blackmail and terrorise a community for a long time.

In aboriginal society nobody ever dies a natural death, death being always regarded as directly or indirectly due to somebody else's spite. Superstitions about the crocodile are almost as numerous as those concerning snakes, chamaeleons, or hyaenas. On the Nile, many peasant Sudanese regard the crocodile as a demi-god, able to forecast and control the river flow, and the reptile plays an important part in the religions of most riverain Negro tribes. The teeth, the scales and other parts are thought by many to have magical properties: the Azande, for example, use the teeth to 'cure' certain illnesses.

When I first arrived in Africa I expected to see crocodiles in every river, lake and stream. It proved to be more than six months before I saw my first, and even then I had only a glimpse as the small reptile sank from sight.

A month or two later I was brought a crocodile, the first I ever handled. I arrived one morning at my field laboratory on the sisal estate to find three strange Africans waiting for me. They had brought a crocodile with them in the hope that I would buy it, it being widely known that I was ready to purchase most animals that were alive and unharmed. The three had come very early in the morning and Kazimoto, when he arrived for work, had told them to release the reptile in the very large rain-water tank outside the laboratory.

This tank stood on supports against the side of the building so that the top of the tank, which was three-quarters full of water, was some nine or ten feet from the ground. The crocodile, so bound with rope and rags that it was almost hidden from sight, had been dumped in the tank still tied up. Fortunately the water revived the animal, which was able to free itself from its bonds.

When I arrived an hour later, Kazimoto told me of the crocodile.

'Go and tell them to bring it to me,' I said, as I settled down to start work. Kazimoto disappeared. About ten minutes later he returned.

'The men say that they cannot bring the crocodile, *Bwana*,' he reported. 'They only caught it by accident in a fish net and are afraid of it. Now that it is free in the tank they won't go near it.'

'Well, it's their crocodile,' I said, 'do they think I am going to catch it?'

'They know that you will if you want it,' Kazimoto replied with candour.

Resignedly I went out. A crowd of some twenty or so *totos* stood around, several labourers and some of my men. The three who had brought the crocodile sat under a tree some distance away. I climbed up on two empty drums, one on top of the other, that were placed by the tank, and peered in, my head and shoulders just over the edge. I contemplated the murky water where at first I could see no sign of life, and then in one dark corner I could just see the nostrils and eyes of the silent reptile. Simultaneously it slid gently below the water. I kept as still as I could on my somewhat precarious stand, and after a minute or two the nostrils and eyes silently reappeared.

I was keen to have this crocodile, being anxious to study it, but I was not sure how I was to get it out of the tank. Cautiously I put my bared arm into the water, moving my hand slowly towards the watching beast, hoping to grasp it by the tail, although the water was too black for me to distinguish its body. In order to reach the reptile I had to lean over the edge of the tank and turn my head sideways to see. Through one eye I could just make out the snout; through the other I could see my audience gaping at me, tense with anticipation, but enjoying it all immensely, probably hoping to see me disappear head first. There was a sudden flurry in the water; I grabbed, missed, and the crocodile vanished again. An 'Eeeeee' of disappointment rose from the crowd when they saw my hand empty, still attached to my arm.

To catch a young crocodile when you have full freedom of movement and the animal is in a confined space is comparatively easy, but in this big, deep tank I was only able to feel about with one hand. Although I did not think that the reptile was more than a few feet long, I did not *know* how big it was, and even a small crocodile has formidable jaws. Each time I put my hand and forearm into the black water I anticipated losing a finger or two. The nostrils appeared again, and this time I nearly caught the animal, but such was its frantic movements and strength that it slipped from my grasp, snapped ferociously, and once again vanished from sight. The onlookers, now doubled in numbers, pressed closer to admire my antics, which, to anyone not knowing what I was trying to do, must have looked quite peculiar.

I made six or seven more attempts but failed each time. On the last occasion the jaws closed within an inch of my hand, and I nearly fell off the oil drums as the beast reared out of the water, such was its panic. The crocodile obviously now felt very insecure, for it had become violent and every time I tried to catch it the tank boomed deeply as either I or the reptile hit the sides. I contemplated climbing in as the water was only about four feet deep but on second thoughts decided against this—the murky water was now stinking as the rotting leaves at the bottom had been stirred up, and the crocodile was agitated and bad-tempered. The tank was not possible to overturn, for it was too big and firmly fixed to the laboratory wall; there was no easy way of emptying it since it was not yet connected to any pipe. We could have bailed it out, I suppose, but it would have taken a long time. The crocodile and I seemed to have reached an impasse.

I jumped down from my perch. 'Kazimoto,' I demanded, as another idea occurred to me, 'go and fetch a pole and some rope from the laboratory.'

Kazimoto returned and I arranged a slip-knot at the end of the stick, planning to put this loop round the crocodile's head. Kazimoto clung to the other end of the tank, which had a slight ledge where he could put his toes, trying with a stout stick to make the reptile head in my direction. The water was now so black with stirred up mud that I could barely see the crocodile's snout even when it surfaced, sometimes plastered with a crown of soggy leaves.

At length I managed to place the loop over the animal's snout and tried to pull the rope taut, but the noose refused to tighten. Yelling at Juma, who was standing below me holding the drums in place, to come up beside me and hold the pole, I took my feet off the drum and balancing with my stomach on the edge of the tank, plunged both hands into the water managing to catch the crocodile round the body. Its additional weight and frantic struggles nearly overbalanced me, and I would have plunged head first into the tank had it not been for Kazimoto who, with great presence of mind, grabbed my feet and held me back.

It had long been a belief of mine that owing to the relatively weak muscles that open a crocodile's jaws it should be easy for a man to hold the jaws together with his hands. It would be seldom possible to do this with a large crocodile owing to the violent movements of the body, especially the powerful tail, but this beast was only about four feet long I had now discovered. Shifting my grip I worked my hands along the crocodile's body and managed to hold the jaws without being bitten.

Several things then happened at once. Jack-knifed over the tank I shouted to Kazimoto, who was still grasping my legs like somebody gripping the neck of a runaway horse, to pull

i

me out. At almost the same instant, Juma, in his excitement, toppled off the oil drum, cannoned into Kazimoto, who let go of my feet as he crashed to the ground. For a moment I balanced over the side of the tank, but the weight of the crocodile tipped the scale and I slid to join it in the water. As I felt myself falling (it happened quite gently) I took a deep breath in order not to swallow any of the filthy water, and closed my eyes. I did not hurt myself except where one of my shins caught the top of the tank, and the next moment I was standing up in four feet of water inside the tank, slime running down my face.

At first I was only aware of the awful smell of the muck that had been exposed and the chill of the water. The next moment I realised that in falling I had lost hold of the crocodile; I must have flung my arms out instinctively to save myself. Somewhere in the confined space of the tank was the terrified and furious reptile. I was very conscious of the vulnerability of my lower limbs at that moment, but resisted the impulse to scramble out as quickly as possible — or perhaps I was too petrified to move.

Fortunately the crocodile rose in front of me; I grabbed it, very relieved to know it was not lurking below. More by luck than skill I caught the reptile by the tail; it twisted round viciously but I caught its neck with my other hand. In a moment I had it helpless, one hand round its jaws and the other holding the tail.

From inside the tank I could see nothing but trees and sky, but just as I looked up I was surrounded by a ring of black faces, each round with apprehension, as Kazimoto, Juma and most of the crowd jumped up and caught the edge of the tank. I started to laugh. Immediately all the faces around crinkled into dazzling smiles, some dropped out of view, and there was great laughing and shouting.

With the help of my men I climbed out, saturated by the slimy liquid and adorned with rotting leaves, but still holding the crocodile. The assembled onlookers fled at the sight as though confronted by a demon, and I could not be sure if this was due to my dishevelled appearance or to the crocodile. Squelching, I went into the laboratory where we tethered the reptile by a short rope round its waist.

When I took the crocodile home the only secure place for it was the bathroom. As a large monitor lizard was already occupying this room I had to choose between them since there was no hope that they would live amicably together, and the monitor had to go. I took it to the dam and released it, watching it race to the edge of the water in a fast, waddling run, plunge in, and swim gracefully out of sight.

The crocodile was soon quite at home and proved to be much less trouble than the monitor which had left scratches everywhere. I found some rocks and sand, and with the bath half-filled with water so that it could lie either on the sand or in the water, the reptile seemed contented. I fed it on pieces of raw meat. After some days it allowed me to handle it without reacting aggressively and on most days I would let it out on the lawn to sun itself. The difficulty was when I wanted a bath. There was no room for both of us, let alone the rocks, so I had to dump the stones on the bathroom floor and deposit the crocodile in the bedroom as it objected to the steam. This involved quite a lot of extra work, for the sand was washed away every time and more had to be obtained. However, it did ensure that the water was changed daily.

One day after my bath I went to fetch the crocodile from the bedroom but it was nowhere to be seen. I hunted quickly through the room, opening cupboards, looking under the bed and so on, but the reptile had apparently vanished. It could not have escaped for there was mosquito-wire over all the windows and the door was shut. It was strange how such a large creature could hide itself, but I had to go out to dinner that night so I had no time to search thoroughly.

It was early morning by the time I drove home. I forgot all about the crocodile and tumbled straight into bed falling asleep at once. An hour or two later I struggled back to consciousness, disturbed by some heavy weight on my legs. Still half asleep, and thinking the blankets folded back at the foot of the bed must have been dislodged, I thrust one foot out of the sheet and sleepily tried to lever the weight off the bed.

The contact of my bare foot with something that felt like cold, rough rock and seemed to be as immovable brought me to my senses like a douche of cold water. I sat up and switched on the light. The crocodile lay across the bottom of the bed and stared back at me for a moment out of yellow, unmoving eyes, before closing them. Its slightly open mouth, disclosing the long, strikingly white teeth, seemed to be smiling in smug self-satisfaction. Where it had been hiding before, and how it managed to clamber up on the bed, was a secret that it kept to itself.

Reaching forward I made to catch the animal, but it surprised me by snapping angrily, its long jaws making an audible click as they closed by my hand. Normally it could be handled without displaying the slightest temper; now it was far from docile and behaving as it did when I first caught it in the tank. Perhaps the fact that it was night made it more active than normal — there seemed to be no other reason for its bad temper. I was only thankful that it had not attacked my foot when I first prodded it. I had to climb out of bed and tackle it from behind, but when I had a firm hold it threshed about madly quite unlike its usual self. I dumped it in the bathroom and went back to bed.

Although inconvenient, keeping the crocodile in the bath worked well for some weeks. I had an occasional visitor who, after being introduced to the crocodile, was quite content to use the wash-basin, but nobody stayed more than one night, even one man who had proposed to stay for three. Later, however, a guest who did not take kindly to my crocodile came to stay for some weeks, and as he was an official visitor I had to rearrange my domestic affairs.

The crocodile, now larger and fatter than when I had first obtained it, had to be removed from the bathroom and tethered outside on the lawn under a shelter. My visitor, who was not an adaptable person and to my mind rather unreasonable, did not like my python, either, and as this, which previously had had the run of the house, kept turning up in the most unexpected places, it had to be put into a large packing case on the veranda. In fact, my guest seemed to dislike all animals even the chamaeleons that lived on the curtains. The crocodile became difficult to look after, and as it was without a pool and had to have buckets of water poured over it several times a day, I took it to a near-by river and let it go.

Chapter 10

CROCODILE'S BROOD

The first crocodile eggs I found myself I discovered by accident when chasing a rare and magnificent mantid on the bank of the Bahr-el-Ghazel not far from Tonga in the Sudan. The river was only a few yards away but invisible as I forced my way along the bank through the reeds and tall grasses, but as I emerged on a hippo path I lost sight of the mantid which flew out of view. Hoping to reach open water I followed the track made by the hippos.

For some reason the character of the vegetation changed; previously I had been feeling my way through stands of ten- or twelve-foot-high grasses growing so closely and strongly that all sense of direction would have been lost but for the nebulous path I made. I emerged from the forest of dark green stalks whose feathery tops shut out the fierce sun into more open terrain with grasses scarcely waist high and here and there a tree set in bare, sandy areas. Along the wide hippo trail to my right, made first through coarse, much spiked grass, then, nearer the river, through *Kurr* grass (*Phragmites*), I could see the glint of water for the first time.

I soon found that there was no hope of reaching open water without wading through thick, glutinous mud that became deeper and deeper. The open water of most African rivers, except where the banks are cleared for villages or cultivation, is often impossible to reach for either there is no definite bank to the slower, broader streams, or else the vegetation is so dense that it is only after hours of labour that the water is reached.

As I retraced my steps the round, water-filled footprints of the hippos, often eighteen inches deep in the soft mud, were difficult to avoid. I noticed the spoor of a youngster each footprint scarcely six inches in diameter. In some places the marks of large crocodiles were distinct in the plasticine mud that took the impression of every animal that passed, even showing the hieroglyph of a ground-beetle that was moving stickily over its surface.

133

Where I had found the hippo path to the river, the ground was slightly elevated, and under a small acacia bush the earth had been disturbed but later compressed as though some animal had been lying on it. With my knife I broke through the hard crust and dug carefully into the moister soil below. As I expected I soon disclosed the white eggs of a crocodile: some fifty eggs were present, each about the size of a goose's egg, laid in the hole scratched out by the female crocodile to a depth of some thirty inches. I extracted two of the eggs to examine at leisure and perhaps incubate, but I carefully replaced the soil.

Since that day I have found a few other nests, mostly in similar situations on river banks in relatively dense vegetation, but once I found three clutches on a river sand-bank devoid of any plant life.

No doubt many factors are involved in the choice of an oviposition site: apart from selecting a situation where the soil temperature and moisture are suitable for incubation, the crocodile shuns those places frequented by man or other predators, and thus would be likely to choose an island sand-bank for preference. On the other hand, its choice must depend on the nature of the river, and many rivers possess no sand-banks but flow for miles through dense, reed-edged banks. Then the gravid crocodile may have to travel some distance inland to find a suitable place to lay her eggs. Nor does the parent, after smoothing down the soil on top of her buried eggs, necessarily mount guard over them. None of the nests I have found has been guarded at the time, but possibly the parent returns from time to time.

It is often said that hatchling crocodiles cannot escape from the imprisoning soil without the aid of the parent. I do not believe that this is true; if it were, then I am sure that the mortality rate would be much higher than it is. After an incubation period of about three months, it would be surprising if all parent crocodiles remembered where they had laid their eggs, or even that they had had any eggs. The young do make a noise, however, that is said to remind erring parents of their duties, and possibly some parents do recall their responsibilities and help the hatchlings escape by digging up the soil above the topmost layer of eggs. I think myself that other adult crocodiles sometimes find the egg-clutches, attracted to them by the smell, or by the snorting and grunting of the young as they try to escape, and unearth them — but to devour the babies, not release them. Certainly when the infants struggle free and reach the water their lives are in perpetual danger from their bigger brethren.

In one clutch that I incubated in captivity, the young emerged without any help from me, although buried under some eighteen inches of fairly compacted soil, which shows that they are at least capable of escaping without help from mama. Hatchling crocodiles are equipped with an 'egg-burster', a spine-like projection on the snout that is lost later, which not only helps split the tough, inner envelope of the egg (the brittle, calcareous outer shell breaks easily as the little crocodile stirs in preparation to emerge) but also to dig their way out of the earth. True, the upper crust of soil may be baked hard, but this is normally a minor obstacle to the frantic pressure of the baby crocodile. After all, many young animals, especially reptiles and insects, are capable of escaping from compressed soil without external aid, often much harder soil than any infant crocodile encounters.

It was not until I went to the Sudan and started my zoo that I kept crocodiles for any length of time; previously I had only kept them for short periods. The nearest crocodiles were at least one hundred miles away from my zoo in Kadugli in the Nuba Mountains, and I had not, at that time, been able to obtain any wild ones. On a visit to Khartoum, I took the opportunity of asking the zoo authorities to give me a couple of young crocs, which they kindly did. Later, I was able to incubate some of the eggs I found and study the babies at their earliest stages.

From Khartoum I had to travel eighty or ninety miles by road to Hassa Heissa, where I was spending the night with some friends, and then I was due to fly back to Kadugli, about three hundred and fifty miles by air.

The two young crocodiles had a safe but bumpy journey to Hassa Heissa in the back of the car, but were parched and covered with dust by the time we arrived. My first thought was to get them into the cool water. My host and hostess were somewhat taken aback when, after my perfunctory greeting,

I asked them to provide accommodation for two crocodiles for the night.

'They're very small,' I explained, 'little more than a foot long and almost at their last gasp. They need a swim badly.'

Wilfred and Elizabeth looked at each other in horror, but concealed their feelings admirably; neither had been close to a crocodile before and, as Wilfred said, they had no desire to become more intimately acquainted; however, for me, they were willing to do what they could. After Elizabeth had produced various tins, all much too small, I tentatively suggested the bath. There was a moment's shocked silence as they eyed one another again, but they capitulated. While Elizabeth carefully removed every toilet article within reach—I do not know if she thought the crocodiles were going to eat the soap, towels, talcum and what-not, or use them for their proper purposes, but she was taking no chances—Wilfred and I let the water into the bath.

I brought in the crocodiles, my hosts looking on from the doorway as I carefully put the lethargic animals in the cool water. There was no reaction at first, but the water turned a sandy brown and then grey as the dust and sand soaked from them. Then all at once they both broke into frenzied activity, half swimming, half skittering, through the shallow water to claw vainly at the sides of the bath. Wilfred and Elizabeth were entranced as they drew nearer to watch, and I had some difficulty getting them out of the bathroom. By the time I left the next morning, Elizabeth was quite sorry to let the crocodiles go, and even Wilfred, although in his opinion I was quite mad, had been pleased to examine them at close quarters.

The pilot of the little Auster aircraft was not so tolerant. He waxed indignant at the prospect of having two crocodiles as extra passengers. After an argument, during which Ken, the pilot, cited various regulations prohibiting him from carrying live animals, painted horrifying pictures of a mid-air battle with two ferocious, man-eating reptiles, and finally said that the aircraft would be overweight if he took them, he was overruled and I climbed on board.

When Ken took off I thought the Auster, which was the smallest of the breed with a top speed of no more than sixty, and which seemed to be all plastic and wire, was going to travel all the way to Kadugli without leaving the ground; but after an interminable bumpy, dusty ride we staggered into the air, Ken looked at me and grinned, signifying that we had only just made it. We flew on to Kosti, landed, and on taking off again we found there was a strong headwind which slowed down the little aeroplane until it seemed almost stationary in the sky. We tried flying higher but the wind was still as strong, and it took us more than double the time to reach our destination. Ken went to sleep on this part of the flight, much to my initial dismay. He had started to nod after we left Kosti, for it was the middle of the day and the heat was intense even in the air. I nudged him awake several times but he only dropped off again; as it seemed to make little difference to our flying whether he were asleep or awake, in the end I let him sleep. The crocodiles became restive, probably upset by the heat. They travelled in the tail just behind us, but there was nothing I could do for them. I had no inclination to sleep at all, with the crocodiles moving about behind and Ken snoring by my side, and the gallant but minute aircraft, scarcely moving against the strong wind, likely to come to a complete halt and drop out of the sky, or even, perhaps, start going backwards. All in all I was thankful to see the hills of the Nuba Mountains below us and to know that I was close to home. This gave me an excuse to waken Ken, who yawned hugely, looked down, and leisurely prepared for landing.

The crocodiles survived the journey without any apparent ill-effects, but it took me several days to recover. Before he left on his return journey, Ken told me that he often fell asleep while flying, but always woke up when necessary. Only a few months later I heard that he was dead, his aircraft having crashed, a total wreck. There was no evidence of the cause, but this was probably the one time when he fell asleep and his sixth sense did not wake him.

*   *   *

My two crocodiles thrived in the pool and enclosure I had built for them. The *Timsah* were a great success with the local people, most of whom had never seen a crocodile. The young reptiles were called *Abu* (father) and *Umm* (mother) for no particular reason except that it was easier to refer to them by some name. They were so alike that it took me a week before I could distinguish them, although Abu was a male and Umm a female. Umm unfortunately died after I had kept her for sixteen months; I had left them in perfect health when I went on leave for three months but, according to the Sudanese keeper I left in charge, Umm swallowed a piece of wire and died as a result. Abu was eventually returned to Khartoum Zoo when I left the Sudan.

I learnt a good deal about crocodiles by keeping them in captivity, observations that could not easily be made otherwise. A newly-hatched crocodile is about ten inches in length, and takes some days to learn to swim properly. In deep, running water the little creature would almost certainly drown. The few I have successfully hatched were given a pool to live in, but clung to the edge at first, refusing to venture into the middle, content to lie half-submerged on the swampy vegetation round the perimeter. Inside two weeks, however, they all ventured into the open water, swimming and diving well. Although the crocodile is equipped with webbed, four-toed hind feet, all four limbs are tucked into its sides when swimming and only the powerful tail is used for propulsion. The webbed feet seemed to be used for turning or for treading water to maintain a desired level.

Of course part of their dislike of entering open water may be due to inherent timidity. The crocodile has only survived as long because it is essentially an aquatic animal, sly and cautious by nature. A terrestrial, carnivorous lizard, the size of a crocodile, could never have held its own against man and would be extinct by now unless protected. Even the largest existing lizards to-day, half the size of a crocodile, are semi-aquatic or amphibious.

Abu and Umm were already accustomed to swimming when I adopted them, although they, too, much preferred to lie all but hidden by vegetation in shallow water, and rarely ventured into the open until they were bigger. Young crocodiles grow quickly, especially if regularly fed, and both Abu and Umm doubled their original length in twelve and fourteen months respectively; in twenty-six months Abu grew from sixteen inches to almost exactly four feet in length, but thereafter his growth rate slowed slightly. After the first five or six years of

life most Nile crocodiles will be between five and six feet, but
later on only a few inches at most are added every year, so that
a saurian of seven or eight feet might be fifteen to twenty years
old. Crocodiles may attain a greater length, but as far as I am
aware there is no authenticated record of any specimen of Nile
crocodile exceeding a length of eighteen feet, although many
people claim to have seen twenty and twenty-five footers. A
crocodile of sixteen feet or over might be seventy or eighty
years old, possibly even older.

Young crocodiles in the natural state feed mostly on insects
and other small creatures. I have watched youngsters scarcely
two feet in length snapping up termites on the surface of a
river, the unfortunate casualties of a vast swarm issuing from
holes near the bank. The young crocs vied with each other, the
boldest even venturing some distance from the protection of
the reedy water in order to reach the termites on the sluggish
surface of the open river.

Apart from any insects that accidently drop in the water,
and it is surprising how many do, the little crocodiles feed on
the numerous aquatic fauna found in muddy reed-beds at the
slow-flowing edges of the streams. Here numerous dragonfly,
mayfly and other nymphs become their victims, as do water-
boatmen, water-beetles and many of the other small inhabitants. Only when it is bigger does the crocodile find such prey
insufficient, and begin to tackle larger animals, at first frogs,
fish-fry, molluscs, crabs, chicks of water-birds, baby monitor
lizards, and even each other; later, when five or six feet in
length, birds and mammals are caught. Birds, as a rule, seem
to form a small part of their diet although there is no doubt
that birds of all kinds may be eaten. It is not unknown for even
a six-foot crocodile to attack humans or other mammals coming to drink.

I fed Abu and Umm mostly on scraps of raw meat placed on
the same rock once a week. After a few months both youngsters would swim to the rock to wait for their meal. They did
not know which day to expect food, of course, but they would
approach the rock when anybody came near. They undoubtedly supplemented their diet with the water-insects colonising
their pool. When they were bigger I began to feed them every
third day, and they came to know not only the place where

they were fed, but also the day and approximate time of feeding. How they did this I do not know: perhaps their stomachs told them.

Little birds, such as cordon-bleus and firefinches, used to come to the crocodiles' pool to drink, especially in the dry season. It was some time before I realised that both Abu and Umm had noticed the birds too. One day I saw Abu stealthily approach a cordon-bleu standing just in the water at the edge of the pool. Abu moved imperceptibly closer, only his eyes showing above the water although the rest of him was perfectly visible for the pool was unpolluted, having been emptied and refilled only the previous day.

As Abu drifted forward, like a water-logged branch in a faint current, it seemed impossible that the little bird could fail to see him. It took no notice at all, however, and Abu slid forward until his head was only inches away, and then, in one fierce, convulsive movement, he lunged forward catching the unsuspicious bird by one flapping wing. It was a near miss and I was amazed at the silly bird, but Abu was out of luck—all he obtained as he withdrew and submerged was a wing feather, and the tiny blue bird flew away with a shriek, no doubt wiser than before in the ways of a wicked world. Subsequently I covered the top of the enclosure with wire-netting so that no more of these friendly and charming little birds should be imperilled.

The crocodiles not only attempted to catch birds. I saw both Abu and Umm chase a swimming lizard across the pool; Abu was the stronger swimmer, but even he failed to catch it in the water; as the lizard, a skink, reached the bank, however, Abu made a great effort and caught its tail; the skink ran on to safety leaving the still wiggling tail in the crocodile's jaws. Lizards were impossible to keep out of the crocodiles' enclosure, and a good many were devoured.

Because they had never had to fend for themselves and were handled fairly frequently, both Abu and Umm became quite tame—or as tame as you can expect a crocodile to be. They never lost their instinct for concealment, of course, and would sink silently below the water when anybody approached suddenly, or plunge into the pool in splashing alarm if sunning themselves on the bank, but they soon surfaced again to see what was going on. Abu (after Umm's death) would always

come to my hand if I put it in the water and splashed
gently.

I never came to feel any real affection for these reptiles, as
I did for so many of the animals I studied, but there is no doubt
that they are remarkable beasts. They are not as strange as the
many erroneous beliefs about them held by people living near
crocodile infested waters, but remarkable enough. Occasionally
curious ideas are even found in scientific literature. For example, before I ever became closely acquainted with any crocodile, I read in a number of books that the upper jaw of this
reptile was supposed to be movable, and, on anatomical
grounds, I could never understand how this could be. When
I came to observe the animals for myself in Africa, it was
obvious that the upper jaw was quite immobile, only the lower
jaw being hinged to the skull. This particular fallacy is easy to
understand, for when a crocodile is lying on a sand-bank with
its mouth open, a common habit, the lower jaw seems to be in
a straight line with the body, flat on the ground, while the
upper jaw is elevated into the air. This position is reached only
because the whole head is tilted back when the lower jaw is
opened.

The teeth of a crocodile are spaced so that they interlock as
the mouth is closed, and they are used solely for seizing or
tearing the prey which has to be swallowed in gulps. As the
gullet is small, the crocodile cannot swallow any large animal,
but has to tear it up first. To do this it needs to obtain some
purchase and has difficulty in tearing up a fresh carcase in deep
water. For this reason it is sometimes thought that a crocodile
will not attack a swimming man in deep water. There is
nothing to prevent the reptile from seizing such a man, however, and pulling him down to drown him — which is, in fact,
what a crocodile does if attacking a swimming animal. Perhaps
whoever evolved the immunity-of-the-swimming-man theory
never troubled to put it to the test. The largest animal I have
seen taken by a crocodile was a dog swimming out of its depth;
it vanished below the surface without a sound. If we had not
been watching the animal from the bank we would not have
seen the brief swirl of water or the long jaws of the crocodile.

The crocodile is able to drown its prey without drowning
itself since the internal opening of the nostrils may be cut off

completely from the mouth by the specially developed bones of the palate. At the same time the external nostrils can be closed. Thus when the reptile submerges, no water can enter the nostrils and the mouth can be held open under water without the water reaching the lungs via the throat. The eyes have a transparent nictitating membrane, with a large lubricating gland, and the ears close at will.

The digestion is rapid, the stomach somewhat resembling the gizzard of a bird with a smaller pyloric compartment leading to the small intestine. The large stones often found in the stomach are almost certainly swallowed to help the animal grind up its food more rapidly. There is no conclusive evidence for this view, but it is difficult to postulate any other reasonable theory to account for these 'gastroliths' — stones often large enough to make it appear that they must have been swallowed deliberately. Anyway, such stones do not appear to worry the crocodile; and other animals, some birds and mammals, are known to swallow stones, presumably for the same purpose.

Ever since Herodotus wrote about them, the Egyptian 'Plover' (*Pluvianus aegyptius*) or crocodile bird has been the subject of controversy. This little bird is supposed to enter the mouths of crocodiles to pick their teeth, but this seems highly improbable. For one thing the teeth of a crocodile, as mentioned above, are widely spaced so that they are not really pickable — no particles of food being likely to remain. All right, says the believer, the bird does not pick the teeth but is after leeches inside the crocodile's mouth. Perhaps, but although I have found plenty of leeches in the armpits and other places on a crocodile, I have never found any actually in its mouth. I have also watched the crocodile birds on a good many occasions, and although they take no notice at all of basking crocodiles, and may wander about amongst them, even hopping on their backs, I have never seen one inside the mouth of a crocodile. The crocodile bird is not only unafraid of the saurians, it is also the last bird to fly away when man comes near. Thus it seems likely that Herodotus and others put one and one together to make a story.

Another bird, the East African thicknee (*Burhinus vermiculatus*), is said to nest for protection in areas where crocodiles bask. It is true that similar forms of protection seem to occur between animals, where one animal is strong, the other weak. For example, some birds habitually nest near wasps' nests, the theory being that the wasps, purely by their presence, afford the birds some protection from predators. In the case of the thicknee I think it more likely that there is no predesign on the part of the bird, the thicknee and the crocodile both happening to occupy the same habitat. The crocodile is found no longer in many places where the bird is still common, yet the thicknee still nests in these areas, it does not desert them.

There is some evidence to show that, under drought conditions, the Nile crocodile will aestivate in holes in river banks or in mud. I have never found such an animal, but since many other reptiles will aestivate or hibernate, it could well be true. That the crocodile will travel very considerable distances overland to find water or a fresh hunting ground, I *can* testify, for I have met them on three occasions.

The first time I saw a crocodile on land away from permanent water was during heavy rain when I was travelling by Land Rover in the southern Sudan. The track was wet and muddy, the country wild and deserted, but the road was not flooded badly. I could scarcely believe my eyes when a big crocodile came waddling across our path. I brought the Land Rover to a slithering halt and dashed out in the pouring rain, as the crocodile disappeared into the long grass at the roadside, but I could not find it. The reptile must have been at least fifteen miles from permanent water.

The next time I saw a crocodile on land was in similar circumstances, except that I was on foot. It had been raining for days previously, but the night was bright and a big moon shone clearly in the rain-cleaned sky, illuminating the tree-strewn landscape and casting deep shadows. With two of my helpers I was searching for snakes. Out of the dark shadows of some bushes, perhaps a hundred yards off, a movement attracted my eye and we saw a long shape detach itself from the shadows. At first I thought it was a great monitor lizard, and ran towards it as quickly as possible, hoping to tree the beast. It was a crocodile, however, and at about the moment I recognised it, the reptile bolted in a waddling run and crossed a moonlit

patch to disappear into deep shadow. By the time we reached
the spot there was no sign of it, but we split up and searched.
One of my men gave a cry as he saw it, but we failed to
catch it.

The third time I was almost lucky but not quite. It was my
first rainy season in Nyasaland, and I had been in the habit of
going out each night for an hour or two to look for frogs on
which to feed my snakes. On this particular night I was alone
although I usually had a man or two to help, for the frogs
commonly found in puddles on the roads were sharp-nosed
frogs — a species that is not only agile, capable of leaping five
or six feet at a bound, but is also alert and slippery. If I had
had somebody to attract the crocodile's attention I would have
caught it.

It had stopped raining only half an hour before I left the
house. I caught a few frogs but not many for the puddles were
too deep. There were numerous river crabs about, for in the
early rains these crabs migrate in considerable numbers at
night, moving along in the streams of water that flow for a
time along the roads and tracks, scuttling across the drier
areas. Some of them must travel many miles carried along by
the flow of water. On this night, too, there were many fish, the
first I had ever seen on 'dry' land in Nyasaland. All the same
species, they were migrating also, wriggling along, scarcely
able to swim in the shallows and where no water flowed flop-
ping through the mud with frantic effort, all following the
direction of the water.

On my return journey I made a detour through the Experimental Station which was just off the main road. On one of
the station roads, only a few yards from the office buildings, I
saw the crocodile illuminated by the headlights, unmoving in
the middle of the road. I stopped the car, leaving the lights on
the reptile, and approached it slowly. Instead of retreating it
stood its ground, body slightly raised on its legs, the head
partly turned towards me. It was not very large, four to four
and a half feet long. As I crept nearer, it brought its tail round
so that the body was in an arc, jaws open, the tail ready to
lash out, in the identical position adopted by a monitor lizard
at bay. I had only my hands to catch it, so I took off my shirt
and wrapped it round my left forearm, intending to ram this

'Snuffles'

5(b) A three-horned chamaeleon

Zanzibar bush
baby

potted eagle owls

5(e) 'Snooky'

6(a) A grey duiker *Sylvicapra grimmia*

6(b) A baby black-ba
jackal pup

6(c) A wild lily

protected arm into the crocodile's jaws, while I caught its tail with my other hand.

I circled trying to manœuvre into a position where I could obtain a grip of the formidable tail with its crest of rough, sharp scales, and at the same time make sure that the jaws would close on my forearm and not my leg or some other part of my body. The crocodile was not co-operative, however, for as I moved round so it pivoted keeping head and tail in an optimum position for use. Eventually the crocodile made the first move, lashing its tail without warning, but not hitting me; as it did so I jumped forward and snatched the tail, obtaining a good grasp. The reaction was as violent as could be, and the animal flung itself about so much that I was forced to let it go again before I could grasp the head.

Instantly it made off in a rapid run and disappeared into some tall maize badly in need of weeding for the grasses were as tall as the maize. Plunging after it through this jungle, I could see the path of the crocodile by the boisterous agitation of the tops of the plants, but then, as I reached the edge of the farm by the main road, I lost all trace of it. Three Africans coming down the road fled for their lives as they saw me come crashing out of the maize towards them, so I had no chance to ask if they had seen the crocodile.

Crocodiles on land are out of their element, and I have no awe of them, but crocodiles in their natural habitat, the water, are a different matter. Then the silent monsters, lurking unseen below the surface, can be terrifying. Apart from highland streams, where there was no fear of bilharzia, the Blue Nile and the Ruo River are the only two African rivers in which I have bathed voluntarily, but I have had to wade or swim through many others when I have been cut off by floods in the rainy season. Fortunately these were mostly seasonal streams not supporting any permanent crocodile population. I only remember one occasion when crossing a river that an alarm was raised.

The sullen water rolled oilily along, like a stream of strong tea. The river was well known for its crocodiles, and the water was swollen to twice its usual depth, reaching well above the waist in the middle of the ford. We were carrying all the luggage over by hand. When half-way across a man suddenly

K

shrieked loudly, lost his head load, and disappeared below the surface; simultaneously an elongate, dark shape reared out of the water beside him, only to vanish again immediately. There was panic as all those in the soupy water struggled frantically to reach the shore. No one gave a thought to help the unfortunate man, convinced as they were that a crocodile had taken him.

Before some of those in the water were able to reach dry land, however, the supposed victim surfaced, and with leisurely strokes regained his footing on the causeway of the ford. Thinking he had been attacked by a crocodile when something struck him and knocked him off balance, he had screamed with fear, but he had only come into contact with a submerged, semi-waterlogged tree trunk. When the porters understood what had happened, they became weak-kneed with laughter, but there was no dallying at the ford.

Another incident that I shall always remember with a smile occurred on the Shire River in Nyasaland. We were planning a trip in a small boat through the Elephant Marsh from Chikwawa to Chiromo. The outboard motor was giving trouble the day before our planned start at four o'clock the next morning. After several trials we were convinced the engine was running fairly well, and Angus and I decided on one more test, persuading Jock, who had been helping repair the engine, to accompany us.

The boat, made of aluminium, was small and light, with a disturbing tendency to rock violently at the slightest movement. Jock was no water enthusiast and had never been known to board any boat smaller than a trans-ocean liner. He also loathed crocodiles with an almost pathological intensity; in fact, his hatred extended to almost any wild animal of any size. He spent much of his spare time with a rifle trying to extinguish as many animals as he could find, although I do not think he ever hunted crocodiles for he would never approach near enough to a river to see them. Why he decided to venture on the water this day remains a mystery, but once convinced that we were only going a few hundred yards upstream, he carefully lowered himself into the bow of the little boat, and we cast off.

A ferry cable stretches across the river at Chikwawa to prevent the ferry, which is motivated by altering its angle to the current, from drifting downstream. When the river is in flood, the cable, which sags in the middle, is close to the surface of the water—even sometimes submerged. Angus steered upstream and we passed below the ferry cable, the engine pushing us along powerfully despite the fierce current until, about ten yards beyond the cable, it suddenly cut out. We lost way, stopped, and then began to drift with the river at an alarming pace. As Angus feverishly tinkered with the outboard, we passed below the greasy ferry-cable once more. As we did so Jock and I stood up and caught the cable to try and stop us drifting further.

For a moment we halted, but the boat was swept away from under our feet; I let go but Jock was left hanging in midstream as Angus and I looked on helplessly. Jock dangled for a moment by one hand, looking frantically about him, and then his grasp slipped on the thick, greasy wire and he plummeted into the river entering the water like an arrow.

We stared impotently at the spot where he had disappeared; the occupants of the ferry, crossing at the time, did the same, only they were open-mouthed with astonishment, while we were shaking with laughter, not knowing that Jock could not swim. It seemed less than a second before Jock's head popped up again close to the boat, for he had been swept along under the water beside us, and, with a desperate fling of his arms, he scrambled aboard, somehow without sinking us although we shipped a lot of water. I shall never know how he managed to do this; he could not swim but fear must have lent him unwonted agility and strength.

We sped on downstream, Jock dripping over everything, muttering gutturally and cursing himself and us, until with a great effort we managed to paddle the boat with our hands to a bank out of the main current. We were several hundred yards downstream. While Jock and I clung to the reeds to prevent us drifting off again, Angus at last started the engine.

It took Jock a long time to recover from this experience, and until he left Africa fifteen months later he resolutely refused any further invitation to go boating.

Chapter 11

BEGGAR-BOY AND BUSH BABY

It was high in the Usambara Mountains that I met the African. He was a sinister figure, his face hideously deformed by long scars and an empty eye-socket, the results of an encounter with a leopard It was only as he passed me on the narrow trail that I noticed he held in one hand a small animal bound in the piece of cloth. I shouted after him and he returned.

'What have you got there?' I asked. For answer he mumbled something, his speech slurred by his torn mouth, and opened the dirty rag.

Inside was a curious little creature, a ball of soft, thick greyish fur, a long bushy tail wrapped round itself, head and legs completely invisible. Carefully picking up the silky bundle, I held it on my open palm to examine it. The animal stirred when I tickled gently with the finger of my other hand, raising its head, disclosing a tiny face with a small mouth and a little black button of a nose, but it did not open its eyes. As I tickled again, I could feel the padded toes moving on my hand, and the long, slender figures gripped mine delicately. Large, hairless transparently-pink ears unfolded and twitched, and then it opened moist eyes wide, staring at me reproachfully through enormous dark-brown pupils, as though about to burst into tears. It was a young galago or bush baby, not five inches long with a six-inch tail.

The owner was quite willing to sell it, and the little animal became mine, the first of its kind I had ever obtained. I neglected to ask the African where he had caught it, but I think he must have found it lower down in the forested foothills for I met him on the crest of the mountain where trees were few.

It was a long way back to my car and burdened as I was with not only the bush baby but a couple of dozen fragile glass tubes full of insect specimens, an Abyssinian slug-eating snake caught on the way up, as well as plant specimens, it was diffi-

cult going back down the stream which was much harder to
follow down than it had been to climb up. All around were
great masses of metamorphic rocks, exposed in peaks, scarps
and small ravines, and in confused dislocation on the bed of the
wild stream, the felosic minerals winking and glinting in the
sun as numerous as the stars in the Milky Way. Other rocks
were sombre and dead in the bright light, or gave sulky
glimmers of hornblende or olivine. Clambering from one rock
to another, plunging through the thin torrent, descending
waterfalls where often I had to make two or three trips to
bring my captives to safety, I wished I had taken an easier
path. However, in two hours I reached comparatively flat
ground and thankfully left the stream to take a track through
the wooded foothills to my car.

When I reached home I was able to examine the bush baby
properly, and it was only then that I discovered it had a
broken hind-leg. It must have been knocked out of a tree with
a stone or stick when the African caught it. That night when
the animal woke up it made pathetic attempts to leap, only to
fall sideways, and I had to restrain it by putting it in a padded
box. I tried to feed it by hand, without much success, and in
the end I caught a number of termites and moths which I left
in the box, first binding its broken leg in splints as best I
could.

It was a wasted effort, however, for when I looked the next
morning the tiny creature was dead, a limp ball of fur curled
in a corner. I believe that apart from the broken leg it must
have had internal injuries. At least it died in as much comfort
as I could give it.

*   *   *

Early in 1950 I first visited Amani, then a Biological and
Agricultural Institute between 5,000 and 6,000 feet high in the
Usambara Mountains, some fifty miles from Tanga. The Institute was established in 1902 by the Germans who built a
light railway there from Tanga, and for many years this was
the only method of reaching Amani except on foot. Now the
railway track has gone and a road follows the old railway bed,
winding rapidly upwards until, in a series of hairpin bends, it
reluctantly reached its destination. At the time of my visit

Amani was still an important centre although now its her-
barium, library, laboratories and staff have been moved.

We found many exotic plants growing at Amani: great trees
planted as seedlings by the Germans, many strange succulents,
beautiful ferns and mosses including a fern-like *Selaginella* with
iridescent greenish-blue leaves and a number of maidenhair
ferns. But the plant that astonished Kazimoto and Jonipayo
was a large bush of the sensitive plant (*Mimosa pudica*).
When touched, the leaflets of this pretty bush close together
along the stem of each branch. I told Jonipayo to touch the
bush with his hand, but he was afraid, not knowing what
would happen. To his distress I took his hand and touched the
leaflets of the nearest branch. As they curled up slowly, Jonipayo changed his moans into a cry of amazement. 'It's alive!'
he shouted, fingering more and more of the leaves until the
whole bush was in a state of collapse. He was so fascinated that
it was difficult to persuade him to come away.

On our way down from Amani that night, just past the little
wooden hut that housed the tsetse-picket in the daytime, a hut
that was gradually disintegrating due to termites, I saw my
first wild bush baby. Only about seven inches tall, the quaint
little creature, ears flattened to the sides of the head and long
bushy tail held high, bounced in four-foot-long hops in front of
the car and into a tree, where it sat on a branch peering down
with great owl-eyes. Watching it in the car lights, I sent Jonipayo up the tree but immediately the bush baby ascended
with astonishing ease, leaping upwards from branch to branch.
There seemed a faint chance of catching it, for the tree was
isolated, and Jonipayo pursued it to the top. The bush baby
looked about, obviously searching for an escape route. It then
walked on all fours to the end of the branch facing the nearest
tree, no part of which could have been closer than twenty feet,
gave a tremendous leap, and just caught the lower foliage of
the other tree. It swayed for a moment suspended by its hands,
and then grasping the branch with its feet it regained its
balance, disappearing into the foliage.

This was one of the few bush babies that I saw in this part of
Tanganyika, for they seemed to be scarce. Perhaps there were
too many predators in the neighbourhood, and certainly I saw
leopards and servals on several occasions, a wild cat once or

twice, while genets and arboreal snakes were numerous. I spent a number of days exploring and collecting in the Usambara range, climbing many of the smaller mountains such as Mlinga, Magoroto (with a road to the top much more hair-raising than the road to Amani), Helogaya and Kjeba. In day-light I searched many hollow trees but I found no bush babies although I unearthed several other animals. The only other time I remember bush babies in the mountains was when I was benighted on the way down after climbing Mlinga.

Mlinga is not a high mountain, only about 3,500 feet, but it is trackless and interesting. I reached the peak late in the afternoon, visibility limited due to the swirling mists. On parting some bushes I was horrified to find that I had not only reached the summit but that there was no more mountain at all—just a sheer drop of hundreds of feet. Two more paces and I should have been over the edge. Clinging to a stout tree, I leant over the precipice. There was no mist, just blurred rocks an infinite distance below. A howling, fierce and very cold wind lashed the rain at the cliff face and along the edge of the mountain, and I was glad to retreat.

Darkness set in before I reached the bottom again, and I had a difficult hour groping my way as the night blackened and the bush closed in menacingly so that I had to stumble along shielding my face from invisible spears and thorns. It was then that I heard the unearthly wailing cry of an unseen galago, aptly named bush baby. The call was repeated many times before I reached the road, and there must have been several present.

Some months later I went to Zanzibar for a few days. Zanzibar Island is not large, only fifty-five miles long and no more than twenty-five miles wide, and situated some ninety miles from the mainland. Although the island is a tourist centre, outside Zanzibar Town, away from main roads and cultivated areas, there is still much to interest the naturalist. The island is flat, there being only one substantial hill, Welezo, which, although under four hundred feet high, seems con-siderably higher since you start to climb from sea-level—especially if you are riding a bicycle on a hot and humid day as I was each time I climbed the hill on several visits to the island.

I spent many absorbing hours on this first visit observing the
wild life. I could willingly sit on a Zanzibar beach for days on
end watching the variety of life on the shore, cooling off in the
warm, sparkling sea when necessary, and looking at the wonderful array of marine animals for the blue waters teem with
life — not only with brilliantly coloured fishes, but with wrinkled
grey or yellowish sea slugs; spiny, worm-like creatures; jelly
fish; anemones in their bright, living colours; medusoids; sea
urchins as prickly as hedgehogs, and sponges like miniature
underwater volcanoes. On the deserted beaches brittle stars
and star fishes, sea lilies and jelly fish, had been washed up by
the hundred, while the shells of molluscs were so numerous in
numbers, shapes and colours that they defied description.

But of all the animals found along this part of the coast
when the tide is out, the various kinds of crustaceans caught
my eye more quickly than any other creatures. Sometimes
crabs were so common that several hundred scuttled away at
my approach, almost rubbing shoulders with one another.
There were several common kinds, most numerous amongst
the rocks and mangroves, but one plentiful stalk-eyed, brightly
coloured crab found on the open beach gave me a lot of
amusement.

These crabs made burrows in the sand, one crab to each
burrow; the tunnel went down about a foot or so and the
diameter of the hole varied according to the size of the crab.
As I ate my lunch under a coconut-palm several of these
creatures were moving about in the bright sunshine. At times
the whole beach seemed alive as they rushed about as though
involved in some complicated dance, flinging showers of accurately aimed sand at one another, but most of the time they
lurked just inside or near their burrows. I watched trying to
understand their curious behaviour. One crab would run
rapidly across the sand to investigate some object, presumably
hoping that it was edible. As soon as it left one of the other
crabs would try to get into the unguarded hole. It was rather
like the children's game of 'twos and threes'. Infrequently the
stranger crab took possession before the rightful owner returned, which, as it careered back across the sand, was met by
a fusillade of sand grains thrown up by the usurping crab and
sometimes driven away. In most cases the owner of a burrow

seemed to defend it successfully except when the intruder was bigger and stronger, able to create a greater barrage of sand-grains, but I never found out what the object of it all was, and the crabs hardly ever came to grips — all their battles being fought at a distance with sand.

It was obvious that the crabs were on the look-out for food and were able to see a small movement some twenty feet away. When I tossed a pebble several would set off after it; the first to reach the stone would pick it up, turn it over and over to examine, before throwing it down and tearing back across the beach to its hole. A piece of sandwich was carried off in great haste as the crab finding it rushed back to the security of the burrow before its companions could attack.

The crabs would even do battle with me. Several times I stalked one to flick little showers of sand at it from a few feet away. Usually it would be backing away from me as I came near, but, feeling the sand grains, the crab would stop and eye me, rising on its legs the better to do so, and then deliberately flick sand back. If I retreated in apparent defeat, the pug-nacious creature followed a short way showering my feet with particles of sand until, satisfied that my rout was complete, it would make off again about its business.

On my second day, on a different beach, I found another animal that really astonished me. I had finished my lunch and walked along the glistening sea-edge of the sands to a cove where the vegetation came right into the water. the waves breaking on numerous rocks. As I scrambled on a rock, a number of small but elongate creatures leapt from some half-submerged boulders into the water; at first I thought they were frogs although I knew of no marine frog.

I sat on the rock to wait with my feet in the water. I did not have to wait long; only a few rolling waves had advanced when I saw several strange, goggle-eyed heads just where the surf cascaded against the rocks in front of me. I then realised that I was looking at some kind of amphibious fish. Floundering about in waist-high water, I splashed from one rock to another in a vain attempt to catch one, but they were far too quick. As soon as I reached a rock where several of the goggle-heads appeared, the fish would be off, skipping effortlessly over the breakers to another rock. I tried creeping up on them, bent low in the water, but they always saw me; I tried rushing at them, but it is difficult to rush successfully through water; I even tried to reach them by submerging in the sea and swimming underwater, receiving only a bruise on my head for my efforts as I collided with a rock, and a graze on my shin when I seemed within inches of grasping one of the fish.

It was not until some weeks later after my return to the mainland that I found these fish again, in much greater numbers this time, for there were hundreds of them on a rocky part of the coast just north of the Pangani sands. With the help of Kazimoto and a couple of other eager youths, I was able to catch two or three, and what curious little fish they were.

I did not know it at the time, but there are perhaps a hundred or more kinds of rock skippers in tropical oceans, all able to shuffle and wriggle along on spray-soaked rocks. The kind that I found* was as goggle-eyed as any and resting on the rocks, resembled a small seal with a frog's head, the flipper-like pectoral fins supporting the front of the body. If one was washed off a rock, which was not often, for the fish seemed to be able to keep its position with astonishing ease despite the often heavy volume of water that flowed over it, the rock skipper would flip away, scarcely seeming to touch the water surface, so lightly and quickly did it skip along, before wriggling up at the edge of another rock. It was rare for one to take the tail out of the water, but sometimes I saw one high and dry but for the waves passing over it every few seconds. These little fish were only about six inches long, a muddy-blue colour, with faint darker bars, and the males had a distinct crest on the head which gave them an even stranger appearance.

In Zanzibar there is varied country ranging from open grassland to dense forest, and in the wilder parts I have walked for hours without meeting a soul. In Jozani Forest I disturbed some wild pigs and collected some interesting ants and beetles, while not far from Mkokotoni I unexpectedly found an enchanting lake, the shore scattered with hundreds of blood lilies or fireballs in full bloom, the vivid red flowers with scarlet stamens showing to perfection against their flat

* *Periopthalmus*, perhaps *P. sobrinus*.

olive leaves and the bright green of the young grasses. Much of the lake itself was covered with the starry, yellow flowers, each an inch in diameter, of a lovely water plant, *Limnanthemum kirkii*, a carpet of deep yellow and green against the still, dark water. A grey heron turned its head to watch me as it stood on the bank, but soon returned to its contemplation of the water as though lost in the beauty of the scene but in reality probably on the watch for a meal. A pair of pigmy geese, the handsome male iridescent bottle-green with a black, white and emerald head, floated near the centre of the small lake.

I found this lake in the late afternoon and leisurely wandered along the bank until nightfall when the air became alive with 'fireflies'. I walked along the shore through the dancing, living lights of tens of thousands of the little beetles, the winking green flashes so confusing the darkness that I had more difficulty in finding my way than if none had appeared.

Later that night I behaved like a tourist and went to see an *ngoma* staged specially for visitors to the island. Surprisingly, the dancers were good, for they were of the Manyema tribe from the Belgian Congo.

The roads were almost deserted as I returned by rickshaw in bright moonlight, the soft clove-scented air now quite chill as the rickshaw-boy sped along on bare, silent feet. As we slowed down at a cross-road, a small urchin full of impudence and hope materialised from the shadows, and padded along beside us, in spite of the gestures and threats of the rickshaw owner. Influenced by the night, and impressed by his persistence, for he ran beside us for at least two miles, I threw him a few small coins. After this, instead of making off with his gains, nothing would make him leave me. He not only followed me back to the hotel, but was there the next morning, and saw me off two days later when I flew back to the mainland. Each night he slept in one of the alleys, for he seemed to have no home.

This vagabond followed me everywhere next day, and I could not shake him off. If I feigned great anger, he would retreat to a safe distance but still followed me as though attached by an invisible rope. In the end I was forced to accept his company for even when I took my hired bicycle and rode furiously away, he turned up panting but still smiling a minute or two after I stopped. That day I made use of him in various ways for, without the least understanding my madness in collecting various *dudus* (insects), he was eager to help in all that I did. He did not seem to have any name, so I called him *Kero*, meaning 'trouble' or 'vexation' in Swahili. That night I paid Kero for his help but told him quite plainly and fiercely that I did not want to see him again. Of course, when I left the hotel after breakfast, he was waiting outside.

It was through this boy, who was perhaps ten or eleven, that I happened upon another small boy — an Indian child this time. Trying to avoid my faithful urchin, I attempted to lose him by dodging into one of the back alleys in the town, off Baghani Street. As I hurried forward I nearly knocked over a small Indian boy.

The child was the only other person in the narrow, crooked alley, and on a string he had a young and very unhappy bush baby; I immediately decided to try and buy this animal, partly because I still wished to keep a galago, and this was the Zanzibar race which I was never likely to have the opportunity of studying again, but chiefly because the creature was obviously quite wretched being dragged along in the hot sun.

The thin Indian boy was not frightened at being bumped into by a strange white man, but just regarded me solemnly with dark brown eyes that in his thin face seemed as large as those of the bush baby. I spoke to him in Swahili, then English, but the child just stood looking at me not a flicker of comprehension changing his wooden expression. He walked off, yanking the unfortunate galago behind him, and I followed, holding some coins under his nose and pointing to the bush baby.

At that moment my little urchin appeared at the end of the alley, saw me, and ran towards us, his black face full of joy at having discovered me at last. For once I was pleased to see him, and in a few words explained that I wanted to buy the bush baby. With an expressive look of 'Just leave it to me' my youthful friend turned to the Indian boy and burst into a torrent of speech. Within two minutes the galago was mine in exchange for two East African shillings, and I put it in my shirt and hurried back to the hotel, Kero trotting delightedly at my heels.

I went straight up to my room and examined my prize. The forlorn creature had lost all its spirit and was bemused by the bright light. I carefully removed the string round its waist, and bathed the sore where the cord had cut into the skin, and then gave it a drink of water which it took thirstily. Putting it in a drawer for safety, I went downstairs again, and called Kero, who as usual was lurking round the hotel steps. I sent him off to buy a banana.

A little time later there was a knock at my door, and a grinning page insisted that I come downstairs at once. At the hotel entrance I found Kero arguing with the large and imposing doorman, the child scarcely able to stand beneath a whole hand of some eighty or ninety bananas! I extricated the boy, placated the doorman, and took my great bunch of bananas upstairs feeling the astonished eyes of some other residents and staff following me, no doubt thinking I must be inordinately fond of bananas. Half-way up the stairs I shed several of the fruit but I did not bother to pick them up. Little Kero, to whom I had given 50 cents (sixpence), had certainly made a good bargain.

I ate seven of my bananas, but could manage no more, and my galago, weak but hungry, nibbled part of another, but I had to bequeath the rest to the hotel when I left the following day. Tearfully Kero saw me off. Not even he could follow an aeroplane. To soften the blow I gave him a pound, but there was nothing more I could do. I never learnt what happened to him; I half expected to see him the next time I visited Zanzibar but he did not appear.

I was a little worried about taking my bush baby back to the mainland; it was unlikely that the customs would make any trouble, but all the same I was taking no chances. I put the animal in my camera case—a leather, rectangular box into which the bush baby fitted snugly—having packed my camera in my suitcase, and put it behind my seat in the tail of the aircraft.

We taxied to the runway where the pilot began to warm the engines. My galago became suspicious at these proceedings, and began to scuffle inside his prison, making muffled but audible grunts and groans. Although there were several other passengers, all were well forward except two rotund Indians in the seats just in front of me. Hearing the strange noises, the Indians turned their heads, four brown eyes regarding me with distrust. I looked blankly at a point just above their heads, refusing to meet their stare. One of them muttered to the other, who shrugged his shoulders. The galago suddenly made a louder noise, a bleating wail. As the heads of the Indians turned quickly, equally quickly I looked back over my shoulder. When I looked round I found the Indians still regarding me, so I said, with a smile, 'Probably a mouse in the baggage.' Whether they understood I cannot say, but they transferred their gaze to some innocent canvas mail-bags stacked in the tail. One of them made a movement to investigate when, to my relief, the aircraft taxied forward again and in a few moments we were airborne. With the engines at full-throttle no other sounds could be heard, and by the time we levelled off my galago must have decided that all was well and gone back to sleep.

When we arrived at Tanga airstrip, I walked over to the customs shed, and was met on the way by Kazimoto and my driver. Nonchalantly I handed over my hand baggage to them, giving the camera case to Kazimoto. While I went into the customs shed Kazimoto went straight to the car with the galago and nobody stopped him. I soon wished I had given him my suitcase as well for I had brought one or two presents on which I had to pay heavy duty, almost half as much as their original price.

Once more, however, I was unfortunate with my bush baby. Its early bad treatment had been too much for it, and despite all my care, it refused to eat after the second day at home, and died two days later.

*   *   *

The sad fate of my first two bush babies deterred me from trying to obtain others for the rest of the time I was in East Africa. When I reached the Sudan, however, I had the opportunity of catching some myself.

The Senegal galago is one of the commonest mammals in the Nuba Mountains in southern Kordofan. In Arabic it is called

Gourdi, or sometimes *Teng*, but being so common and well-known to all the Nuba tribes it is known by many local names.*

The first time I went out at night in my car, I was driving back from Talodi, some sixty miles from Kadugli where my home was. We had not travelled many miles when we saw the red tail-light of a car in front. This was strange for there was never much traffic on that road even in the dry-season in daylight: this was the early wet-season and night time. From time to time the red tail-light disappeared, only to reappear a mile or so further on. I was driving fast and I could not understand why I had not caught up with the vehicle in front.

The solution came when, at a bend in the road, we saw the red light go floating through the air away amongst the trees: what we had mistaken for the tail-light of a car was the reflection from the large eyes of a number of bush babies one after another along the roadside. At a distance the reflections exactly resembled the size and colour of a rear-light, but as we closed with the animal the reflection ceased suddenly as though the car in front had passed round a bend to be hidden from view. It was only the bush baby that created this confusion, for there was no other animal in the area whose eyes reflected light in the same manner. Genets, often up trees, and civet cats, for example, have eyes that reflect a yellow light, while the red eyes of nightjars, another common sight at night, were too small to be mistaken for the rear-light of a car. Large emperor moths or hawk moths that settled on the road at night had eyes giving a surprisingly large red reflection that we sometimes mistook for nightjars, but never for a bush baby.

Before I attempted to catch any bush babies for my zoo, I spent a good deal of my spare time observing them in their natural surroundings. At that time I had to travel at night quite frequently for my car, a Ford Pilot, tended to boil in the daytime while the petrol vapourised before it reached the engine. At night this happened less frequently, and it was not until later that I obtained a Land-Rover, a more suitable vehicle for the Sudan. As we travelled I made a

* For example, *Ka-ta* by Kadugli Nuba, *Ka-da* by Miri Nuba, *Fordona* by the Abu Sinoon and Kanga Nuba.

note of the number of times we saw the reflections of bush babies' eyes, and so soon discovered where they were common. Although galagos occurred throughout the Nuba Mountains and in many places to the south, they preferred living in sandy or *gardud* (a gravelly soil formed by weathering of rocks) areas, probably because the trees growing on such soils provided the best food and shelter.

There had to be hollow trees, however, or hollow branches, for the bush babies rarely hid elsewhere by day, preferring as a rule thorny, pinnate-leaved trees. On nights with a full moon we rarely saw a galago. Whether this was because there were few insects on such nights, or because of the danger from predators or some other reason, I could not be sure. In cold, windy or wet weather, too, the small mammals remained snugly at home. This considerably restricted observation for it was only on calm, still dry nights with at least a quarter moon that I normally saw them. They were probably most numerous on calm moonless nights, but of course then there was not enough light to see them.

I knew from experience that galagos are creatures of habit, usually active about half an hour after sundown although when the full moon rises early they may wait until after the moon has set. I first realised this in Kenya some years before, where a friend had a family of wild galagos living in a tree in his garden. Promptly every night half an hour after sunset the family would leave their nest in the hollow trunk, taking the same route through the branches for, like monkeys, galagos always seem to follow a set pattern, leaving and approaching their sleeping place by the same branches.

Only a few miles away from my house I chose a grassy termite mound as my vantage post; here I could lie at full length without being seen, yet at the same time I had an unrestricted view of several trees, occupied by at least two bush babies, there being a large sandy clearing under the trees. There was a tedious wait before the first animal appeared, although I could hear them moving before I could see them. At last one came in sight, leaping on the trunk of an acacia tree.

At first I could not make out what it was doing clinging to the trunk like a squirrel. After a minute it dropped to the ground, and began to eat something held in its hands. After

7(a)

...cks in Mkulumuzi Gorge

7(b)

7(c)

8(a) Cave entrance Mkulumuzi Gorge

8(b) Bat Hall caves

nibbling this, the creature took fright suddenly at some imagined danger and with long, rapid hops, crossed the sandy area, bounding into a tree. I discovered later that it had been eating a piece of resin that had oozed from the bark; this was an interesting discovery for I had not realised before that bush babies ate the gum from trees, no account that I had seen mentioning this important fact. I soon found that gum was one of the chief items of the diet.

A short time passed before another galago, or perhaps the same one, came into view on a low branch a few yards away; it was silhouetted against the sky picking at the bark with one hand, and now and again popping something into its mouth. In daylight I had noticed that this tree was infested with termites, the earthen covered ways running to the topmost branches, and the galago was breaking open the tunnels and catching the termites with delicate fingers as they scurried across the gap. For the next half an hour I caught glimpses of the bush babies, but by this time ants had discovered me, so I left.

I watched bush babies on several nights over the next few months; sometimes I spent an hour or two without seeing one; on other occasions I saw as many as five or six. As well as the gum, they ate all kinds of insects, often hunting diligently on the trees for grubs, spiders, beetles and termites. Once I saw one turning over small stones on the ground in the manner of some monkeys; this, however, must be rare for they do not often descend to the ground to feed and I could never persuade any captive to turn over stones for food. They frequently picked off loose pieces of bark to reach insects below. They nibbled the young shoots and growing-points of various plants, and ate the fruits or seeds of many common trees and shrubs. I once saw one in a cotton field eating the petals of cotton flowers, and in captivity galagos sometimes ate the immature seeds of cotton bolls. They were very fond of the fruits of the *Heglig*,* and when such a tree was in fruit it was rare for the bush babies not to find it. The fruits of the *Homeid*,† of the *Ardeib*,‡ and the flowers of wild *Acacia, Bauhinia*, custard-apples, and *Hibiscus* were other favourite foods.

* *Balanites aegyptiaca.*   † *Sclerocarya birrea.*
‡ *Tamarindus indica.*

L

Although I did not see any wild bush baby capture a lizard, there is no doubt that they will chase nocturnal geckoes, and in captivity one captured and ate a gecko that ventured forth to feed on insects at a light. The bush baby seemed half afraid of the lizard, although it snatched it up with lightning speed; having done so, however, it snapped it in two as though breaking a twig, and threw it down again. While the maimed lizard wriggled convulsively, the galago just looked at it, but when it was quiet the bush baby picked it up and ate it. Carrion is also eaten at times, as are fledgling birds, when the head is usually bitten off, although the Senegal galago certainly kills far fewer birds than does its bigger relative, the thick-tailed galago, that is as big as a domestic cat and as bloodthirsty. The thick-tailed galago has a more restricted distribution than the Senegal galago, however, and does not occur in the Nuba Mountains.

Perhaps the most interesting experience I had when watching bush babies in the wild occurred about a year after I arrived in the Sudan. I had found a fairly isolated *Heglig* tree in fruit, and wanted to see what would happen to the fallen fruits. I knew a bush baby was living in the tree, so I spent part of three nights lying in wait.

Several raids had been made already on the fallen fruits, for many of the rounded, oblong, greenish-yellow drupes with the sticky, date-like flesh round the big seed, had been nibbled by rodents and porcupines; obviously, too, the red hussar monkey had visited the tree. Hundreds of fruits remained, however, scattered in a wide circle under the canopy.

I made myself as comfortable as possible on a branch of a near-by tree, equipped with a cushion and my binoculars. Within a few minutes of darkness, the first visitor arrived — a black-backed jackal, treading delicately like a gazelle, pausing now and again to sniff the air suspiciously. He was in beautiful condition, the black stripe on his flank and his deep black brush velvety in the twilight. Satisfied that there was no immediate danger, the jackal, resembling a small alsatian, began to eat the *Heglig* fruits, sometimes using his paw to roll over a fruit half hidden in the soil or under leaves; at one point he scratched vigorously at the ground, apparently in an effort to extract some insect. For some five minutes I watched before he made off, probably alarmed at a slight movement I made to ease my cramped bones.

The next arrivals were quite different, a fat little hedgehog trundling into view, followed by two miniature editions, the white bands on their faces distinct even in the dim light. All three began to waffle and sniffle as they found the fallen fruits. The parent nibbled one or two, but the youngsters just seemed to snuffle around without showing any real interest in the fruits. Obviously the adult hedgehog was not particularly interested either for within a minute or two she moved away on her short unseen legs, closely followed by her offspring in single file, three spiny balls rolling over the sand and short grass.

So far there had been no glimpse of any bush baby although it was quite light with a three-quarter moon sufficiently strong to cast grey shadows but still low enough in the sky to light up the ground below the tall *Heglig*. I was just thinking I would leave when a bush baby bounded into the moonlit arena. It sat down purposely, picked up a fruit and began to eat, nibbling rather like a squirrel holding the fruit in both hands and turning it round in its paws to eat the succulent flesh. As soon as it had devoured one, it moved in ungainly fashion on all fours, its bottom high in the air due to the length of the hind feet, found another fruit, and squatted on its haunches again to devour it.

I was pleased I had waited long enough to confirm that a wild bush baby would eat *Heglig* fruits, for although I knew captive ones would eat them it did not necessarily follow that the *Heglig* was included in the diet of feral ones, and no amount of observation of captive animals compensates for even a moment's view of the activities of a wild one.

The next night I drew almost a blank, for the only animal I saw was a female duiker which was very nervous, and only stayed long enough to devour two or three fruits before she bolted away again, her hump-backed form, with head held low, jinking across the open ground like a large, panicky hare.

On the third night of my watch I was lucky to see part of an interesting drama. The moon was now almost full, the sky cloudless, so the whole ground was brightly lit — enough light to read typewritten print. Two bush babies were feeding on the ripe fruits on the ground, and from my position about seven yards away but above them in my tree, I could see every detail; I also caught sight of another movement to the left of the galagos but further away from me. Cautiously I turned my head thinking at first that the movement was that of a snake, but it was a genet, crouching low on the ground.

The bush babies, not sensing the cat's presence, were quite unconcerned. Although their sight is remarkably good, bush babies are probably at a considerable disadvantage on the ground, for being only small animals their vision must be very limited except when in trees.

I kept my eyes on the genet, which seemed intent on capturing one of the bush babies. Its reddish-yellow, black spotted, weaselly body merged extraordinarily well against the background of gravelly soil sparsely sprouting short grass and young weeds. Inch by inch it edged forwards, scarcely seeming to move but drawing perceptibly nearer to the bush babies, cleverly making use of the small hollows in the ground and the shadows. Despite its painfully slow, cautious approach, it seemed impossible that the lively, alert galagos would not see it on that bare ground, but it crept nearer and nearer, a solid shadow that seemed to drift along.

I must have shifted slightly, for I snapped a small dead twig. The genet froze; the bush babies each soared into the tree with great leaps. The genet, unable to contain itself when it saw its dinner making off, went in open pursuit up the trunk almost as quickly as the galagos.

Jumping out of my tree, I ran across to the *Heglig* into which all three animals had disappeared. Shining my flashlight upwards, I soon discovered one bush baby; it stared down for a brief second with its great, round eyes, and then leapt away silently. The cat was clinging to a branch high up the tree, but of the other bush baby there was no sign. Hoping to catch the genet, I called to my men waiting in the Land-Rover some distance away. When they ran up, I told Adam, a lanky youth, to climb up the tree while the rest of us stood at the bottom.

Keeping my torch on the animal which had not moved despite all the commotion, or perhaps because of it, I directed Adam, for he was unable to see it as he climbed. When at last

Adam was a few feet away from it, the cat flung itself out of the tree, much as I had expected, and fell almost at my feet. Before it could recover, I caught it by the body, missing the neck. The next moment it had sunk its teeth into my hand, but I managed to clasp the neck with my other hand, freeing my lacerated fingers. One of my men rushed up with a sack; I dropped the animal in; streams of blood gushed from my wounds, but I was very pleased to catch the genet so easily.

Chapter 12

MORE BUSH BABIES

S o o n after my preliminary observations on bush babies I decided to examine by daylight all the hollow or partly rotten trees in a suitable area. I took Younis, my chief assistant, and his brother, Badr, with me to a place where previously we had marked some dozen trees as suitable for investigation, and now we were going to see what they would produce. We knew that at least two of the trees were the homes of bush babies, but it was likely that we would find other animals, too.

The first two trees produced nothing of interest. The third tree was perhaps twenty-five feet tall, with numerous holes up the trunk, the bole being completely hollow. It took twenty minutes to block all the holes except one at the bottom and another at the top. With plenty of dry grass Badr lit a fire at the bottom hole; as soon as it was burning well he put green grass on top which produced a dense smoke. Very shortly afterwards the first wisps of smoke appeared at the top of the tree, and soon the smoke began to pour out thickly until the tree resembled a factory chimney. A moment later a bush baby crept out, spluttering, and began to crawl along a branch. It was an easy matter to catch it. On the ground the animal gave a kind of hiccuping cough two or three times, and sat blinking in the sunlight, confused by the light and making no attempt to escape. This was always the case with this strictly nocturnal animal when caught in the daytime; occasionally one might hop off, but always clumsily, as though blind.

I was pleased to make such an easy capture, but I did not like this tedious method of capturing animals; not only did it take up too much of my very limited spare time, but any animal present was liable to suffocate since it could not always find the way out of the tree, being disorientated by the smoke. Bush babies, particularly, disliked leaving the darkness, and sometimes refused to move. This happened at the next tree. Although we sent clouds of smoke through the dead trunk and we could hear the galago moving inside, it would not or could

not escape to the outside. We put the fire out. Although hollow
and mostly dead, the tree was lithic in its hardness as we found
when we tried to chop it down; it would have taken hours
using only a *panga*, all we had, so we gave this bush baby best
and passed on to the next tree.

It was not until we had smoked four or five more trees with
only one result—a large rodent that fled before I could identify
it—that we made our next capture. This was, surprisingly, a
ground squirrel or side-striped squirrel,* another common
mammal of the Nuba Mountains and, since it is diurnal, often
seen. About eighteen inches long, this squirrel has a whitish
stripe down each side of the sandy-brown coloured body, and
eyes ringed with white hairs. The ground squirrel, as its name
suggests, is a terrestrial beast living as a rule in burrows in the
soil, so when one shot angrily out of the hole high up in the
tree we were unprepared for it.

The squirrel, chattering in alarm, left the tree so quickly
that it missed its footing and went sprawling, head over heels,
to the ground. Without loss of momentum, and uttering a
high-pitched cry that is seldom heard except at moments of
great fright, it fled across the ground, the sparsely-haired tail
fluffed out to the fullest and flicking in all directions as it ran.
Younis, with great presence of mind, chased it from the
moment it landed but although he twisted and turned in the
track of the bounding animal, he had no hope of catching it
as long as it kept running. Fortunately the squirrel took refuge
in a hole in a termites' nest, giving us all time to arrive in
pursuit.

After some minutes' digging we could see an inch or two of
brown fur amid the crumbling grey soil of the termite mound.
In the arid, almost tangible, heat, when to touch a sunny rock
surface could result in blistered fingers, movement of any kind
was intolerable, let alone chasing madly after animals. I sat
down, soaked to the skin, perspiration falling like raindrops
from my body but evaporating immediately on reaching the
ground. In heat of this sort I would not have been astonished
to hear a hiss as each droplet of moisture expired on contact
with the baking soil.

Directly I sat down, Younis and Badr did the same. The

* *Xerus rutilus.*

squirrel made no movement. The problem was now to get it out without damaging or losing it. From experience we knew that to catch it by hand was to invite some vicious bites. Despite the razor-sharp teeth I was willing to take the risk rather than lose it now, for I had only one specimen in my zoo, but again I knew from past attempts how difficult an adult ground squirrel was to hold. The short, bristly fur on the tight skin somehow enables the animal to slip from even a firm hold so that it was like trying to catch a large, active fish. Stupidly —in such heat one is sometimes almost as bemused as a bush baby in bright light—I did not think of the net which we had left not far away.

Before I made any decision the problem was solved for us. We were still sitting under the sparse shade of a *Kadada* bush looking at the termite mound when the squirrel began to move again. To our astonishment it wriggled out slowly, backwards, dislodging loose chips of the outer rock-hard soil that we had broken. With hair fluffed out and standing almost on end it seemed unaware of us. When free from the soil and before it realised the danger, I jumped forward, catching the squirrel by the neck so that it was unable to bite. In a trice we had it safely tied in a bag that Younis was carrying attached to his shorts.

I was puzzled by the squirrel's behaviour, so unlike its ordinarily agile, exuberant movements. It had seemed to be alarmed at something in the termite mound, and looking closer at the opening we had made, I saw some of the inner, loose rather moist soil moving slightly. With my sheath-knife I gently scraped this away, instinctively pulling my arm away as a snake struck at the blade. As I did so a very violent saw-scaled viper crawled into the open, hissing and rustling its scales against each other, and repeatedly striking at random as it crawled towards me.

This small viper, almost certainly the Asp of Cleopatra, is a highly venomous, often aggressive snake, probably responsible for the greatest number of fatalities from snake-bite in the Sudan. With the curious sidewinding movement typical of it when aroused, the viper moved over the hot sandy soil, the high temperature activating it to such an extent that it appeared frantic. Five or ten minutes' exposure on that hot soil would have been about the limit of its endurance before it died—held still, it would have been dead in two minutes. I cut a stick and with this held the snake's head down while I picked it up by the tail, releasing its head at the same time. Scarcely two feet long, the viper wriggled so violently that I was afraid it would break its own back, but it had no chance of biting me since I held it at arm's length, and, despite its contortions, the head could not reach my arm or body.

We had no other bag handy, and rather than carry the reptile by its tail back to the Land-Rover, a few miles, I took one of Younis's stockings. He was barefoot, having left his shoes in the car, but he had stuffed his stockings in a pocket of his shorts. With considerable difficulty I guided the viper into the stocking, which I tied in a knot at the top, leaving a few inches free as a handle, and we started back to the Land-Rover with our captives.

We had not gone far when Badr, behind, shouted '*Umm Shedigat! Shedigat!*'

I looked back: the lad was right; there on the ground was another saw-scaled viper wriggling under a bush. I was amazed to see it, for on such a hot day, this viper, like any other animal, barring a few foolish men like us and some insects, normally concealed itself until dusk when it was cooler. Perhaps we had disturbed it as we passed.

It took nearly an hour to catch it, for we were now on a clay pan, criss-crossed with great fissures, and the reptile had entered a deep crack near the bush. Eventually we dug it out. I took Younis's remaining stocking, and secured the second viper. Then we set off again, stopping to retrieve the other stocking and the sacks containing the bush baby and the squirrel, dropped in the excitement. It was then I discovered that we had only one saw-scaled viper after all. Younis's first stocking had a hole in the toe, and the supposed second snake was the original one that had escaped to lead us a fine dance! Although the second stocking did not seem to need mending, I tied the foot as well as the top into a knot.

*   *   *

Apart from the bush baby caught with the squirrel, I found only three or four others by smoking them out of trees when looking for other animals. When I wanted to obtain a number of galagos for my zoo, for study in captivity, and to breed, I caught them by another method, the best and quickest way I discovered to obtain live bush babies without injuring them.

The basic idea was to go out at night with a spot-light and flashlights, drive along slowly, and try to catch any galago seen. At first I had little success, but gradually, as we became experienced, and I gathered together a team of eager youngsters, I could go out on any suitable night and guarantee to catch three or four in two or three hours.

Not that I required so many for my zoo, but later, when I was asked to collect bush babies (thought to be possible reservoirs for yellow-fever virus) by the Medical Department, it was possible to send them several. A few months before I finally left the Sudan, the local Sudanese doctor, and the Provincial Medical Officer, an Egyptian, came and begged me to collect as many bush babies as possible to send to Khartoum. I was not happy about the wholesale collecting of these attractive and harmless little mammals, but they promised that they would be well looked after, it being only necessary to obtain blood-samples from them. I took Younis and his gang with a Land-Rover and we caught five, but later I sent Younis and the men by themselves since I did not have time to go, and they collected a couple of dozen. In fact, all the bush babies for research at the Wellcome Laboratories in Khartoum were collected by us, although the doctors took all the credit!

Our first successful hunt was on a still, dark moonless night when I took with me Younis, Badr and five or six other youths, all in their teens. None of the youngsters was paid for this work. They came along partly for the excitement, and partly because they were all younger relatives or friends of Younis, and people in the Sudan were brought up to do what their elders told them.

The boys piled into the open back of the Land-Rover, stripped right down by removing the cab and windscreen, Younis sitting on the bonnet with a powerful flashlight, while Badr sitting beside me operated the spot-light. We took no nets. About a mile from Kadugli we saw our first galago. However, this one was in a tree close to a number of others, and we did not waste time trying to catch it, for in such a situation the bush baby nearly always escaped by leaping from tree to tree. Many lived in thickets of thorny trees, too, and these we generally avoided, the trees being difficult to climb. We were looking for galagos in fairly isolated, preferably unarmed, trees.

The third bush baby we saw was in a suitable tree. Badr kept the spot-light trained on the animal, I drove almost under the tree, while Younis and the boys jumped out before the Land-Rover stopped, dashed over and surrounded the tree. Ali, our best climber, lithe and light, almost as agile as a bush baby, started to climb. Noiselessly the bush baby leapt higher but the beams of light followed it. Ali followed until the animal took refuge in the topmost branches as he began to shake the tree. This always had the effect of making the bush baby either fall to the ground or cling closely to the branch it was on. If it did not fall, the climber went higher and could often catch the animal before it recovered sufficiently to leap away.

In this case the violent movements of the thin twigs to which the galago clung soon dislodged it to fall right into the hands of Younis, who popped it straight into a sack. This was lucky, for more often the galago fell to the ground, recovered before anybody could catch it, and went bounding off pursued by several boys. Occasionally it escaped to another tree, but often it was caught before it had travelled very far. Given a clear run, a fleet youth could catch a bush baby without much difficulty, for, despite the long hops of the animal, it is not very fast and soon tires. No galago we caught was ever hurt by falling from a tree but I preferred to catch them in the branches.

Making a lot of noise was quite important if we were anxious to catch galagos only. Bush babies become confused by loud noises, and the shouting and unearthly howls produced by my gang were enough to frighten themselves, let alone a bush baby. A galago has very sharp teeth and is capable of biting fiercely and painfully, but our captives were often too confused and dazed by the noise and the suddenness of the assault to attempt to bite.

We caught another bush baby in the next half an hour, and I found that it was a female, like the first. It was important therefore to obtain a male.

We did not have to examine the next one to tell it was a

female, for she was carrying her baby. I stopped for a time to watch, but prevented the boys from catching her. Naturally a galago with young is easier to capture for the mother is less active when so encumbered, but there was always the danger of causing the animals some injury by chasing them about so I left unmolested all females with young. Until old enough to forage for itself, the baby is carried underneath its mother, clinging to her fur. Watching this one in the lights, I was astonished at the way she managed to leap from branch to branch despite her burden, the baby spreadeagled against her chest.

The next galago we caught was a male which reproachfully regarded me with great, sad eyes as I was examining it in the headlights, and then, without warning, turned its head right round like an owl, and without malice sank its teeth into my hand. The wounds were a nuisance for the rest of the night since whenever I moved my hand they bled afresh.

We now had two females and one male, and could have gone home, but we were having such success that I went on. We caught another male, and then we found another, a female carrying twins.

Most galagos produce only one young, but two are some-times found, Altogether, during five years, I found eight cases of twins, six in the wild and two in captivity. There was even one case of triplets in captivity, but these were still-born. As far as I am aware triplets have never been recorded before in a bush baby. Even with twins, the mother has great difficulty in getting about; I am quite sure no galago could cope with three babies at once.

We watched the mother and twins for a little while. She was unable to jump, for the babies were quite big and she could hardly carry them. She simply clambered about from branch to branch. After a few minutes she disappeared into a hole in the trunk, and as it was now after midnight, we returned home with our four captives.

*　　*　　*

The four bush babies settled down well in captivity. I found that one of the females was gravid, so I kept her in isolation. The other female and one of the males seemed to be quite happy together despite the lack of formal introduction, so I kept them in the same cage. The second male I put in a cage by himself.

Unlike some of the other one hundred and fifty animals I had at that time, the galagos were easy to feed, eating almost anything that was not noxious. Despite their catholic feeding habits, I soon found that all bush babies were not alike. Later I had as many as a dozen bush babies at one time and I found that while most would eat nearly any kind of cultivated soft fruit, including temperate fruits such as apples (which, in the dry season, I obtained occasionally from the north), one specimen I had absolutely refused to eat oranges although others liked this fruit. Another disliked rice although it would eat a little now and again. Most biscuits were eaten with relish, but one galago always made a face if given a ginger-nut, which was acceptable to several others.

In order to make sure that the galagos had enough insect food, I tried putting a paraffin pressure-lamp just outside the cages at night. The first time I did this the bush babies were very upset and refused to emerge from their sleeping boxes. Now and again one would put its head out, and then retire again, muttering to itself. Their grumbles were the first sounds I had heard them make since they had been in captivity. Although bush babies are capable of making a considerable variety of sounds apart from the wailing cry normally associated with them, they were silent when they knew they were being watched.

The next night I had the lamps put in place and watched from concealment. The same thing happened at first, but after half an hour or so of muttering and peering from their boxes, one galago braved the light, and emerged. I think it would have been some time longer before any ventured out had it not been for the considerable numbers of insects flying round the lamp.

The first galago to step into the light proceeded cautiously over the ground on all fours and not attempting to leap, but in a minute it was jumping about catching insects and cramming them into its mouth. Within five minutes all the bush babies were out feeding. From that time on, as soon as the lamps were in position just out of reach outside the cages (for the galagos would have been burnt if they had touched the lamps), all the bush babies would leave their sleeping quarters and hopefully sit around waiting for the insects to arrive.

On some nights when very few insects were attracted to the lamps, the galagos would express their disapproval by hopping madly about from branch to branch in their cages. As with other food, they were selective and refused many insects — particularly those moths, grasshoppers, beetles and bugs with nauseous, poisonous or irritant properties.

Some time later, having been away for three weeks, I went to visit my four galagos. To my surprise only two, the male and the female sharing a cage, were to be seen. Then I was astonished to see another bush baby hopping across the grass to the cages where it began to catch insects, but using only one hand to do so. As I approached it hopped off quickly, taking refuge in a *Neem* tree growing in the zoo garden.

I opened the sleeping box of the second cage, and found it empty. The solitary male bush baby had escaped through a hole in the netting, and the one I had seen coming to feed at the lamp was obviously my erstwhile captive. When I questioned Hamad, who looked after and fed the animals, he told me that the bush baby had escaped three nights previously and he had been unable to catch it. He also informed me that the pregnant female, in the third cage by herself, had given birth to twins the previous day and this was the reason why she was not outside the sleeping box.

It was disappointing not to have been present at the birth. I looked into the sleeping box, and there she was, the two tiny babies clutched to her as she lay curled on her side in a corner. I let them be. Bush babies bear their young in nests in hollow trees, and I had provided her with leaves to make a nest. She had used the leaves and some of her own fur to line the wooden box.

The next night as I watched for the errant bush baby he appeared again soon after the lamps were lit. This time I was ready; Younis placed himself between the bush baby and the *Neem* tree in which it had made its home, and I managed to net the flustered animal. I found that one hand was quite badly burnt, this being the reason why it was using only one hand to catch the insects at the light. I kept the animal until the hand was properly healed, and then let it go free again in the *Neem*.

Releasing it into the tree was as good as keeping it caged, for it was still in the zoo compound and I could watch it when I wished. It stayed in the tree for more than two months, apparently sleeping in a nesting box that I had put there for birds months previously, but one day it disappeared and I did not see it again. It seemed likely that it had decided to find a mate, for, just before vanishing, it was very friendly with the female that had produced the two young. The free male sat close to the wire of her cage and chattered to her, but she took no notice of his attentions, which was perhaps why he took himself off.

The mother bush baby was very attentive to her two young. She suckled them and carried them about for almost six weeks. During the time she carried them, she still came out quite regularly for food, although for the first three days she scarcely moved even inside the box. When the youngsters began to forage for themselves, it was a pretty sight to watch them trying to imitate their mother. At first both were very clumsy, and to see them trying to catch moths was very funny, with the mother sitting near by watching their efforts. They learnt quickly, however, although one was more adept than the other.

They soon found that all insects coming to the light were not good to eat, and pulled horrible faces when biting a distasteful moth by mistake. Learning was not entirely a matter of trial and error, however, or entirely mimicry of the mother. Certain brightly coloured moths — *Arctiidae*, or tiger moths, for example — were ignored right from the beginning seemingly by instinct, but perhaps due to their smell. At first, too, they were frightened of big moths, such as big hawk moths or emperor moths, and fled to their mother when one of these came to the light, but later they grew much bolder.

In the beginning the mother did not carry both babies together every time she emerged from the sleeping box, for on several occasions I saw her with only one baby at her breast. But she returned frequently to the box, and I suspect she took them out in turns. When the babies were three months old and had been foraging for themselves for a month or more, I took them out of the mother's cage, putting them in a separate cage where they thrived.

I could not establish the exact gestation period, even though I managed to breed some bush babies in captivity. My original male and female pair I kept for nearly three years, and they produced one young, but, as in the case of another captive pair, I could not be sure when they mated. In the wild, bush babies seemed to mate most of the year round, but October and November were probably the peak months. The gestation period is between six and eight weeks, young being most frequently observed in December and January.

Experience soon taught me that it was unwise to put more than two bush babies in the same cage together if they were strangers. One day I caught a new bush baby and, having nowhere to put it alone, I placed it in a cage with two others that I had kept for some months. Returning in the evening, from some way off I could hear an angry chattering and now and again a loud croaking cry. I found quite a row in progress. The three bush babies were all in the open part of the cage and angrily shouting at each other; now and then one of the two original inhabitants put out a hand and caught hold of the newcomer, pulling its hair. They reminded me very much of two small boys ragging a new pupil at school. I watched them for a few moments, but when the quarrel seemed to be getting out of hand, the two combining forces against the newcomer, one holding and the other biting, I intervened.

*   *   *

The very human antics of bush babies and the fact that they are so common in the Nuba Mountains, has resulted in a wealth of folk-tales concerning them. In the vast Sudan where communications were poor, where strife and warfare dislocated life even in recent times, where illiteracy was the rule, the story-teller came into his own. Even to-day, especially in the more remote places where books, newspapers, cinemas and other forms of recreation do not exist, the village story-teller provides an irreplaceable form of entertainment for people whose lives during British rule were often dull. Independence brought its own excitements, but I am sure that the teller of tales still flourishes.

A story told by the people of Korongo Tabanya concerns
the origin of wrestling, which is the national sport of the Nuba.
The naked wrestlers usually adorn themselves with wood-ash
to help absorb the sweat.

A man from the village of Korongo Tabanya was walking
along a path early one morning on his way to his field of *dura*,
when he came on a gathering of all the animals in the neighbourhood. He hid and watched them and, to his amazement,
he saw them wrestling with each other, one pair after another.
Eventually the hyaena had beaten all the other animals, and
was proudly boasting of his skill and strength when, skipping
along a path towards the gathering, came a little bush baby
who had not heard of the wrestling competition.

All this the Tabanya man saw, but then he heard the hyaena
growl to the galago (for this was in the days before the animals
had lost the power of human speech, so my informants said),
'I have wrestled and beaten all the other animals in the world.
Come here, Bush baby, and I will wrestle with you and beat
you.'

The little bush baby stopped and sat on his tail. He thought
awhile, as the Tabanya man in hiding could see. The bush baby
was obviously frightened of the great hyaena, but then he
seemed to have an idea.

'I cannot wrestle with you on the ground, O Father of
Hyaenas and Champion of All the Animals,' the bush baby
squeaked (saying in an aside, 'except me'). 'However,' he continued, 'if you will come up into this tree, Father of Warriors,
I will wrestle with you there.'

The hyaena did not like this idea much, as the Tabanya man
was quick to observe, but he was too full of pride and confidence, and thought he could beat this tiny creature in any
situation: besides, the other animals were watching. So, with
great difficulty and much groaning, the hyaena climbed up
into the tree. The galago leapt up after him in a single bound,
sat on a tiny twig, and shouted, 'Come on, then, you *toosom-
boosom*!' (a Nuba term, 'chuckle-head' being perhaps the
nearest translation).

The hyaena was so incensed at being called a *toosom-
boosom*, that he jumped at the bush baby, but as he did so,
the little galago leapt to another branch in a twinkling of an

M

eye, and the silly hyaena fell heavily to the ground, very badly frightened, for he thought he had been thrown there by his opponent, and ran away. This is the reason why the hyaena always cries at night, and is never seen by day, for he is ashamed of his defeat by a tiny animal and dare not be seen by the other beasts. This is why, too, the hyaena has to feed on the leavings of others, for his defeat turned him into a great coward.

The Tabanya man returned to his village in great excitement, and related to the wondering villagers all that had happened. The men of the village decided to hold wrestling matches like the animals, and began to challenge men from other villages and hills. They say in Karongo Tabanya that the defeat of the hyaena by the bush baby is the reason why, if a man covers his face, arms and chest with white wood-ash, and goes naked to see a galago in its hole in a tree at night, the bush baby will think he has come to challenge it to a wrestling-match, taking it as an invitation for the next night (for bush babies are never punctual). The bush baby is so proud of having beaten the hyaena that it thinks it can beat man as well.

After the man has gone, the bush baby will go to all its relatives in the vicinity, and tell them to gather together in readiness. The next night, if the man returns, he will find dozens of bush babies eagerly awaiting his arrival. These can then be caught easily, and taken home to make a fine supper for the man and his family. I must admit that I never tried this method myself!

Another curious belief in the Nuba Mountains is that if a bush baby happens to bite a *local* man, it will never let go until it hears a zebra bray! This must be an old tale, for there are no zebras in the Nuba Mountains to-day, so it would seem that any Nuba unfortunate enough to be bitten would have to travel a hundred miles or more to find the nearest zebra to release him! How does such a belief originate? I certainly do not know. There are many such tales in Africa, when one animal is associated with another in some absurd manner, yet this is one of the strangest for there seems not the remotest possible connection between zebras and bush babies. Perhaps someone just made this story up as a joke which has persisted in the simple minds of his hearers.

Yet another belief, a more logical one, is that if a bush baby is captured and kept in a hut it will take the first opportunity of putting its tail in the fire, and then, with flaming tail, will bound all round the hut to set it alight and escape. This tale possibly has its origin in the fact that it has been known for a man to take revenge on an enemy — without fear of discovery — by tying dry grass to the tail of a bush baby, setting the grass to smoulder, and releasing the animal near his enemy's hut. The galago would leap about and with any luck, jump on the hut, setting it alight. An ingenious, if cruel, form of attack.

Chapter 13

GREAT SNAKES!

APART from insects, probably my greatest interest is in reptiles, which have always fascinated me. As a boy I kept all the British lizards and snakes as well as some foreign ones, but it was not until I was fourteen that I obtained my biggest snake.

I bought this reptile from a pet shop but they did not seem to know what kind it was and I was not able to identify it. It was not a python although non-poisonous. I used to call it a black rat snake, for the proprietor said it fed on rats and milk, and that it came from India, although I told him that no snakes drank milk and I suspected the snake to have come from southern Europe.

My snake was four feet one and a half inches long, grey-black in colour, with beautiful yellow eyes. I took it to school but, after enjoying several days of secret worship by some dozen boys in the know, and a pampered, frog-fed, but somewhat dull existence, to my great grief, it escaped.

The snake's freedom lasted for months and it terrorised the school, for although it found its way into the foundations of the old building which had wooden floors and was full of hiding places and rats, it was not content to stay out of sight, and kept appearing, to everyone's consternation. One maid had hysterics and fled precipitately, never to be seen again by us.

As far as I know, the cook was the next person to see it. She was made of sterner stuff, and in any case she had only time to fling a saucepan at it before it slithered into a hole in the skirting — luckily she missed. Collapsing on a kitchen chair, her great bulk enveloping it like a feather mattress, she panted indignantly about the 'great ugly brute' that she, for all she was born and bred in the country, 'had never seen the likes of before'.

For a week or two nothing further was seen of my snake. Then we learnt that one of the masters had seen it, and thereafter we noticed that they walked in and out of the Common Room, past the place where the reptile had been, either very warily or very quickly, according to temperament. One of the more athletic teachers took to carrying a hockey-stick about. But although I spent all my spare time trying to find my snake, I never saw it again and it was not re-captured.

A year or so later the pet shop proprietor, knowing me to be a good customer even if a python priced at thirty pounds was well beyond my means, allowed me to handle a reticulated python that was four times my length. I never forgot this early experience, even after ten years and a world war, but it was not until I reached Tanganyika that the opportunity occurred to catch my own pythons.

*   *   *

My first view of a wild python came about quite accidentally when I was with Tommy and Jim, two young Agricultural Officers, by the Sigi River. I had been only a few months in Africa, Jim about the same time, but Tommy had seen two rainy seasons and so was quite an old hand. Tommy was helping me to collect some termites, when Jim, who had wandered away, ran up and began to stutter. We regarded him with some concern. It was the middle of the day and scorching hot even in the shade of the riverain forest, and Jim seemed incapable of coherent speech, but, with boggling eyes, pointed to a bush near the river bank. We stared but saw nothing, and Tommy took Jim by the arm.

'Come on,' he said, 'you'll feel better if you sit down.'

Jim found his voice. 'Let go, you fool. I think there's a damn great snake under that bush.'

I hurried over, the others following more circumspectly. The bush was bowed down with a mass of vegetation bound together with passion-flower vines, the ends of the branches touching the ground, forming a black hollow, like a cave. Through the dark opening I could just see the python, ten or eleven feet long, I suppose, although I could not distinguish head or tail.

It was no good attempting a direct assault, I thought, for the snake was bound to make off into the river flowing on the other side of the bush, so I decided to try and station myself between it and the water while the others drove it towards me. I put this plan to Tommy and Jim, who were cutting them-

selves a stout stick apiece for self-protection, and, unenthusias-
tically, they agreed to help.

'You're quite sure it's not poisonous?' Jim whispered
anxiously.

'If it comes towards me,' threatened Tommy, 'I'm going to
bash its head in, poisonous or not.'

'You can't do that,' I exclaimed, horrified, 'I want it alive.
When I get between it and the river, just lob some stones or
poke it with your sticks; it's bound to make for the water.
Whatever you do don't hurt it though.'

'I'm more worried about it hurting me than I am about
hurting it,' muttered Tommy.

I hoped for the best, and walked upstream a little way before trying to reach the river to work my way back between
the snake and the water. The bank was covered with the
vegetable equivalent of a barbed wire entanglement, and five
minutes later I was thoroughly imprisoned up to my waist in
sharp spines and prickly branches, my flimsy clothing giving
little protection, and I was streaming with sweat. Tommy and
Jim were hidden from view. At last I reached the river, and
made my way along the edge of the bank above the water until
I was opposite the python's lair. My position was far from
secure, for I had to cling to trailing roots and branches and
dig my toes in the soft earth of the almost vertical bank to
maintain my footing. I was not sure how I was going to catch
the great reptile if it came out, but it was the best situation I
could find.

'All right,' I shouted, 'try and chase it out.'

I heard a confused mumble in reply, and then all was quiet.
I waited until my toes began to feel cramped.

'Hurry up,' I shouted again, 'I can't stay here much longer.'

There was a startling splash behind me. Carefully I turned
my head to look, but only widening ripples marked the surface
of the stream. A croc? A monitor? Two crashes in the vegetation in front, and I realised that Tommy and Jim must be
throwing stones towards the python and one had overshot into
the river. I clung on and waited.

Almost at once the python lunged out of the shrubbery
about two feet away. Supporting myself by a thick branch I
made a wild grab and caught it near the tail as it dropped

down the bank into the river. For the moment I held on but I could not lift it back up the bank. Then the big snake found purchase with head and neck round some reeds at the water's edge, and there ensued a tug-of-war, the snake trying to pull itself free, while I tried to pull it up the bank.

Something had to give, and to my annoyance it was the branch that I was holding with my other hand. Falling down the bank after the python, I managed to grip a root and only my feet entered the deep and fast-flowing river, but of course I lost the snake. I watched regretfully as, swimming under-water with only ripples to show its progress, the reptile van-ished rapidly downstream.

I retraced my steps through the thorny vegetation, and emerged, shaken, scratched, bleeding, with torn shirt and muddy feet. Jim and Tommy looked at me.

'No python?' Tommy said.

'No python,' I agreed.

'Good,' said Jim with satisfaction, 'I was afraid you might have expected us to help you carry it.'

*   *   *

The failure to catch this python only made me more de-termined than ever to find one to photograph and study at close quarters. But I had little spare time for snake-hunting, and although I offered a high reward for a live python, I could not induce any African to catch one.

Eventually it was Tommy who found a small specimen about seven feet long, when he was supervising a gang of labourers. They were about to kill it violently with sticks and stones when, hearing the rumpus, he managed to stop them.

When I examined the reptile it did not seem to have any serious injury but was very torpid. I had nowhere to put it for the night except an old sack that I put under my bed. Even if the snake escaped it could not get out of my room, but I forgot to warn the servants.

The next morning I was awakened by a scream and the crash of crockery, my early morning tea. Opening my eyes I was just in time to see the bare legs of my servant, Ali, dis-appear round the door. I felt under the bed; the sack was empty. The python was coiled in the middle of the floor, pear-shaped head lifted enquiringly as it stared in the direction of Ali's retreating form.

As I dressed, furtive sounds near the door attracted my attention; peering in were three open-mouthed black faces, Ali having brought the cook and gardener to bear witness. The python, which until now had not moved, decided to inspect further. With a graceful, slow-motion it lowered its head and glided forward over its own coil. The three faces abruptly vanished and the slap of bare feet on the stone floor receded in the distance. I shut the door, putting the snake back in the sack, and placed a table leg on the edge of the bag where the reptile had forced a hole in the threadbare hessian. Then I went to breakfast.

That afternoon I intended to take some pictures of the python in the sunlit sitting-room, and Tommy, Jim and a young man called Peter, all came to 'help'. We moved all the furniture to the walls and I tipped the python out in the centre of the floor. Tommy stood behind the settee; Jim in a corner, prepared to defend himself with a broom, while Peter nonchalantly settled down with a newspaper.

The python, hissing gently, uncoiled itself from the undignified knot it was in, and slithered cautiously over towards Peter's chair.

'Aren't you afraid of being bitten, Peter?' Tommy asked, from his position behind the settee.

'Of course I'm not,' said Peter, glaring over the top of his paper.

'Then why are you holding that paper upside down?'

Peter hurriedly left his seat as the python wound itself around the chair leg. With an effort, I levered it off, putting it back in the centre of the floor. For the first time the snake began to get angry: sides heaving as it hissed heavily, an ominous sibilance that spread, almost as tangible as steam, through the air. I should have let it calm down before I went on my hands and knees in front of it to take a picture, but I wanted it coiled to strike. The head was not quite at the right angle, and I stretched out my hand to attract the python to make it turn, but I succeeded all too well, for in a flash the mouth gaped and the python struck.

In my preoccupation with the camera, I was not quick

enough to avoid the bite and the python gripped my hand between my thumb and forefinger. Instinctively I pulled my hand away; I knew that it was the wrong thing to do but the reflex could not be controlled. The sharp teeth lacerated the back and palm of my hand, leaving two embedded in my flesh. Blood poured from the wounds making the injury look much worse than it really was. Only when I came back after washing my hands to show minor scratches did I convince my friends that I was not maimed for life. Eventually I was able to take a series of photographs, including some close-ups of the head while I sheltered behind a cushion to prevent further mishap, but when the film was developed I found all our efforts had been in vain, for in spite of the apparent brightness in the room every frame was dreadfully under-exposed.

The sequel came a few days later. Tommy strolled in to see me.

'There's a football match to-morrow and the staff are playing a side that always wipes the floor with them. The men want your help.'

'I'm not going to play football if that's what you're after.'

'They've more sense,' Tommy said rudely. 'It's not that; it's your reputation as a wizard. They want you to put a spell on the other team. Give me something I can tell them is a powerful *dawa*, it'll encourage them no end.'

'That's all very well. I could easily mix up something, I suppose. Even turn them blue or green, if you like, with one of the dyes I'm using to mark insects. But supposing it doesn't work? Or supposing they win hands down? They'll pester the life out of me for spells. Anyway, I don't really approve of encouraging these beliefs.'

'All right, all right. You won't encourage them; they'll believe it anyway. The other team have a witch-doctor and our men say that is why they always lose.'

'Well, surely our team has a witch-doctor, too?'

'That's the trouble. He's no good. They think you're a much more powerful wizard, especially as you lived after being bitten by the python.'

I was rather sensitive at having being bitten, since it was my view, and still is, that no hepetologist should ever be bitten by his charges, any more than a chemist should blow himself

up by mishandling his chemicals. Ever since the python episode my own household staff as well as most of the Africans on
the station had been expecting me to drop dead at any time.
My servants, who had watched the whole incident through the
window, had no doubt embellished the affair. The fact that I
was able to kill insects with milk (which is what an emulsifiable
insecticide resembles when mixed with water), went prowling
about at night, collecting animals, had no fear of snakes,
chamaeleons or other dangerous beasts, lent substance to my
increasing reputation as a witch-doctor. The station Africans
were an unsophisticated, credulous people.

In the end I decided with Tommy that he would tell the
team I had treated the pitch with some powerful magic to
make their opponents slow. I did not see the match, but the
following day Tommy came round to see me.

'Well, how did it go?' I asked.

'Very well. It was a draw. It's the first time they've played
this team and not been beaten. They told me that they
thanked you very much.'

Even Tommy sounded surprised at the result.

'Are you sure that you didn't do anything to that pitch?'
he said.

                    *   *   *

When I finally caught a python myself it proved to be extremely docile. It had been found in a chicken-house, the owner
of the hens walking ten miles to tell me, in a state of great
excitement and indignation that a great snake was devouring
his birds and would I please do something about it. On reaching the village, the headman informed me that the snake was
really a demon in disguise, sent by a witch-doctor commis-
sioned by an old enemy of the hen-owner. It was impossible to
kill or catch.

With some trepidation I crawled into the small, dark,
smelly opening of the wattle and daub hen-house, for although
I presumed I was looking for a python I was not certain. The
descriptions given me by the villagers were so imaginary that
they were of no help. The snake could equally well be a cobra
or even a mamba. While I did not mind being confined in a
dark and narrow space with a python, I did not relish tussling

with a cobra or mamba under such conditions. At that time my experience of cobras in the wild was limited to a single encounter which had not been entirely successful, and I had yet to meet a mamba.

As I crouched just inside the entrance it took several minutes for my eyes to readjust to the gloom after the intense sunlight, but at last I could dimly make out the interior. The hen-house was divided into three sections, one large central room about four feet high and eight feet long, and two smaller compartments on either side. I found the snake, apparently fast asleep, in the corner of the right-hand room. To my relief it was a python. The entrance to this compartment was only about a foot square, the floor sticky with droppings and quite disgusting, so I crawled back to the entrance to ask for a sack to lie on.

'Hallo,' I called from within the gloom, 'fetch me a clean sack.'

All I could see of the crowd outside were bare legs, which now scampered in all directions as everybody fled in terror at the sound of my voice. I had been so long without a sign they were convinced it was the demon-snake talking to them. I was forced to go into the open again before anybody would venture near; once convinced I was alive after all, I was given a sack to lie on.

Inside once more, I half wriggled through the inner entrance. The python stirred, and I could see the bulge in its middle caused by the meal of the previous night. Lying at full length I caught the reptile round the neck, grasping the tail with my other hand before it had time to do more than hiss enquiringly. In this position it was helpless, but it was a laborious task to drag the heavy body through the small opening and into the open air.

The gasp of amazement from the crowd soon turned to wild jubilation at the overthrow of such a 'redoubtable' enemy. The python retaliated by regurgitating a hen at the feet of the nearest villagers.

When alarmed all snakes may regurgitate their prey, a fact that has led to the erroneous belief that a python will cover its prey with a slimy saliva before swallowing it. The stench of a partly decomposed regurgitated victim is one of the worst smells I know, and I quickly moved away, carrying the python over to my car. On the way the reptile sicked up another hen, and half-way home it regurgitated a third hen on the floor of my vehicle.

*   *   *

There are some seventy known species of pythons and boas in the world, but apart from the small boas of Madagascar and the sand boas of north and north-east Africa, the only members of the family occurring in Africa are the African python (*P. sebae*) and the royal python (*P. regius*). There is said to be a third kind in Angola but this is unlikely to be distinct.

The African python is by far the largest snake in Africa, and about the third largest in the world. When many Europeans (to say nothing of other races) start to talk about snakes they can put even the most Munchausenian fisherman to shame, and the size attributed to pythons would surprise even a Texan.

Python skins may be stretched (if this is done very carefully a skin may be lengthened by at least as much as a third again) but not as far as the truth may be after a few whiskies. The maximum known length of an African python is twenty-four feet: a length formidable enough to satisfy any reasonable person, one would think. Specimens of eighteen or nineteen feet have been found recently but are sufficiently rare to cause some excitement, and to-day any python exceeding fifteen or sixteen feet is exceptional.

In spite of man, the African python is still not uncommon in many places even if it rarely attains the age and size that it may have done in the past. There may well be remote areas where the snake may still attain a great size. In such little known regions as the Sudan--Ethiopian border south-east of Malakal, the west bank of the Nile above Fashoda, the Bahr-el-Arab, in parts of Equatoria and Bahr-el-Ghazal Provinces, the upper Pangani River and other East African streams, in places on the Great Lakes, and elsewhere in some of the wilder, well-watered parts of northern Mozambique, Kenya, Uganda and the Congo, I have seen pythons and believe them to be still common in such areas where it would not be surprising if monsters of twenty or more feet still occurred.

Strangely, it is not always a rare snake even in some densely populated places if there are wooded streams. On the lower Shire River in Nyasaland, for example, where the human population is as dense as any in Africa outside the towns and considerably greater than in many parts of rural England, I have found the African python to be as common as in similar places without human inhabitants, although the largest I found there in three years was only thirteen feet long, and it seldom survives to attain even this size.

In sixteen years in Africa I have personally caught thirty pythons of more than five feet in length, many smaller ones, and I have seen dozens of others. Apart from two that I gave to the Khartoum Zoo, and with the exception of two or three injured ones, I let those captured free again. The largest of these, fifteen and a half feet long with a maximum circumference of twenty inches, I caught in the southern Sudan. It was a very easy capture as the reptile was crossing the road at the time; the only trouble was to lift it into the Land-Rover. It was so heavy and awkward that it was as much as two of us could manage, and as fast as we pushed one part of the body in so another part pushed itself out again.

The largest python I have ever seen in Africa was again in the Sudan, in the Eastern Jebels of Kordofan. I heard of this giant just too late to save its life, and by the time I reached the village it was already dead. African pythons are not common in the area, although the more docile, handsomer but considerably smaller royal python is ubiquitous, and it was unexpected to find this one so far from any large body of water.

It had consumed two goats the previous day, a nanny and an almost grown kid, and then hidden under a bush but a few yards away from the scene of its crime to sleep off its gargantuan meal. The incensed owner of the goats and his friends soon found it, and were busily engaged in skinning it when I arrived. It was not possible to measure accurately but it was at least eighteen feet long. The Nuba offered to sell me the skin; I told them had the python been alive I would have bought it from them, but as usual they were horrified at the idea of trying to catch one alive. As the goats, whole and undigested, but covered with mucus, were removed from the stomach amid sickly stench that polluted the hot air and mingled with the acrid odour of the naked, dung-smeared warriors, I left the Nuba to their unpleasant task.

The normal expectancy of life for an African python may be no more than about ten years, chiefly because of man who kills it whenever possible, although its life potential is at least three or four times this. In captivity, one has lived for twenty years, other pythons for more than thirty years. Like all snakes it is capable of surviving long periods without food; in fact, given water, the python can live as long as three years without food. One specimen I kept refused all food for fifteen months before breaking its fast by devouring a dove that had been living in the same cage for two months, the python hitherto ignoring the bird. Thereafter, it ate regularly, but sometimes a captive will starve to death unless forcibly fed.

The African python will eat almost any live animal ranging in size from a tadpole to a large antelope, but naturally the prey depends on the size of the snake and availability, larger pythons living almost entirely on warm-blooded animals. The most usual victims are birds and moderate-sized mammals, while domestic hens, goats and dogs are commonly attacked in populated rural districts. Occasionally a python will make an unusual meal or encounter an animal that is too much for it. There are records of fights between pythons and crocodiles, for example, and they have been known to attack porcupines, but I have never witnessed such incidents. One would be inclined to think that a porcupine makes an uncomfortable meal, but pythons, like most snakes, tend to swallow their prey head first, so that as it was ingested the quills of a porcupine would be forced flat.

The Nuba of southern Kordofan keep domestic pigs, a small, black, hardy race half the size of those on an English farm, and I recorded one case of a pig being swallowed by a python. Normally these active pigs kill every snake on sight, and like all pigs have a high resistance to snake venom, but the non-poisonous constrictor is obviously a match for one, at least sometimes.

It was a considerable thrill when I discovered my first python's eggs, for they are rarely found. The greyish, soft-shelled eggs, about the size and shape of a table-tennis ball, were in moist soil below a *Tukku* bush (*Grewia*), twenty-six in all, not far from the swamps known as Lake No. The parent python had obviously chosen her site with care for the eggs were laid in a slightly elevated place where there was little danger of flooding. The soil, friable humus, was not reached by the direct sunlight although the sun's rays filtered through the bush for part of the day.

Since then I have found several clutches, all except one in similar places, and all screened from direct sunlight. Once I was fortunate enough to see a female laying her eggs at night. It was difficult to see much, but she scooped out a hollow with her snout, pushing away the soft soil with head and body. After some ten minutes' work, she carefully deposited her eggs in the hole, and smoothed the soil back again by pushing it with the weight of her body, using her head to level the ridges, spending a long time arranging it to her satisfaction. The hollow she made was only shallow, eight or nine inches deep, the soil above making a small mound when she had finished.

It is said that a python will often help to incubate her eggs by coiling round them, her body temperature increasing at this time, but I have not found the parent on any clutch that I have discovered. Possibly she incubates the eggs thus when conditions for hatching are not very suitable; in captivity, for example, or in more open areas where the humidity is less and the soil liable to dry out more quickly. Or she may stay with her eggs to protect them from predators, particularly from monitor lizards and various small carnivorous mammals, although I have never seen this myself.

The highest number of eggs that I have ever found was thirty-seven, the average per clutch being about twenty-five, but rarely clutches of over one hundred have been recorded. I only removed two of the clutches that I found, but I managed to rear a few of the eggs. Some appeared to be infertile, while the rest went mouldy. The five newly hatched young averaged twenty inches in length and were active almost at once. I fed them on tadpoles and young frogs, on small pieces of raw meat, and soft-bodied insects, all of which food they ate readily.

Young pythons seem to be sexually mature in two or two and a half years, and, in my experience, attain a length of six or seven feet in four to five years. It is probable, therefore, that a python of fifteen feet would be of the order of twelve or fifteen years old, the rate of growth decreasing with age — of course, there is no hard and fast rule since many factors influence growth.

Pythons are amongst the easiest of wild animals to catch in the open away from dense bush or water. Usually when disturbed their one object is to get away, but after a meal they are often so sluggish that they make no attempt to escape or defend themselves. An active python, cornered, may strike repeatedly and the bite is painful but easy to avoid, and even the largest python is no match for a grown man who does not panic and uses his intelligence.

When a python attacks a large mammalian prey, a goat or duiker, for example, or even a carnivore, its success in overcoming its victims depends to a great extent on surprise and on terror. As a python attacks a large animal from concealment, surprise is almost always achieved. It strikes with gaping mouth, the numerous, recurved teeth, longest at the front, holding the prey firmly with an unexpectedly strong grip. Often the blow from the lunging head knocks the victim off-balance, and the snake is quick to encircle the prey which is frightened into frenzied struggling and rapid, deep breathing. At every breath the captive exhales the python tightens its coils, until the animal, unable to take sufficient air, suffocates. If the prey did not struggle and breathed normally, the python would probably not be able to subdue it at all. In the very remote eventuality of a grown man being attacked by a python and finding himself trapped within the coils of the body, he would have to be careful not to breathe deeply, while considering means of freeing himself.

As far as I am aware there is no record of an African python having killed an adult person, but people have been 'attacked'. This charge is a bit unfair to the python since in such cases the human always seems to have been the aggressor, although perhaps unintentionally. To approach a python closely might constitute 'aggression' as far as the snake was concerned, and the reptile might then strike out in self-defence. Of course, some people only need to be startled by a snake and will call this 'being attacked' even though the reptile has disappeared in a second or two. There are at least two authentic cases of young children being killed by pythons, however; whether by accident or design is a moot point, but a small child passing close to a large and hungry python would prove, I imagine, quite a temptation to the beast.

Chapter 14

THE ELUSIVE PYTHON

THE only time I had any real difficulty in catching an African python was in a remote, uninhabited place west of Lake Abiad (Abyad) about half-way to Abyei on the Bahr-el-Arab. Numerous *Tebeldi* or baobab trees grew in this region of flat, well-wooded grassland. Having left Tanganyika, I had been in the Sudan for a couple of years, and I was making a survey of the alternate hosts of various insects, chiefly cotton-stainer bugs and bollworms of cotton, the baobab being one of the chief hosts of the former insects.

I had two assistants with me, and other staff working elsewhere. Younis, my right-hand man, accompanied me everywhere during the years I was in the Sudan, and he proved even more valuable an ally than Kazimoto had been in Tanganyika. Badr was a younger half-brother of Younis.

We came to one huge baobab and found it was hollow, as these trees often are. Entering the cool interior through a hole in the trunk at ground level I saw, to my surprise, a large python resting on the ground. I backed out quickly, hoping I had not disturbed it, and called Younis and Badr who were some way off. Although I had examined some fifteen hundred baobab trees in which I had discovered quite a number of different animals, this was the first time I had found a python in one.

When Younis and Badr came up, I left them outside to follow the python should it evade me, and I went back into the trunk through the inverted V-shaped opening, but the python had already gone. We all searched the gloomy interior. which was like a large room, for the bole was more than sixty feet in circumference, but the reptile was nowhere in evidence and must have climbed up into the honeycomb fibrous matrix that still filled the rest of the trunk nine or ten feet above our heads. Looking up we could detect a faint glimmer of light that we discovered filtered through the fibrous matter from a hole in the bark twenty-five feet up.

I was very keen to capture this python, for at that time I had only one small African python in the zoo that I had started at Kadugli about a year before, although I had several royal pythons. I thought that perhaps we could flush the snake out from the top either by climbing through the upper hole or by using smoke. The difficulty was that the lowest branches, which were alive despite being hollow, were fifteen feet up; there was a massive limb just below the upper hole, but there seemed no way of reaching it. The Land-Rover, that I often used as a ladder, was several miles away.

After a vain attempt to scale the smooth trunk, we did an acrobatic act. I bent over with my hands on the trunk of the tree; Younis climbed on my back, followed by Badr, by far the lightest, who stood on Younis's shoulders; after teetering for a moment or two, Badr managed to reach the lowest branch and swung himself up. He climbed cautiously higher, for baobab trees are notoriously treacherous to climb, even large branches being liable to snap almost as easily as a stick of celery.

Badr peered into the hole but could see nothing. I was anxious to get up there myself, for Badr refused to feel about with his hands in the hole in case the python, having made its way up through the inner fibre, was close, but even standing on Younis's shoulders I could not reach a branch.

We threw Badr a long stick which he poked down the hole while I waited inside the trunk, but apart from a few fragments of the fibrous inner tissue, nothing appeared. We then passed him some dry grasses that he placed in the hole, set alight, putting green leaves on top to make a smoke. I went inside the hollow bole again, and after a few minutes a wisp or two of smoke appeared but no python. To be effective the fire needed to be below so that the smoke would be drawn upwards, but there was danger of roasting the snake alive if we did this. I called Badr down and concocted a new plan.

Inside the bole, Younis climbed on my shoulders. Badr handed him a stick, which Younis used to poke at the layers of dry pith above him. A thick flotsam of fibrous particles fell each time Younis prodded, and occasionally a large chunk came away. After a minute or two an extra large piece of the light, dry pith fell away, and all was confusion. The python had fallen with it and landed on Younis, clinging desperately to his shoulder with its tail wound round one of my arms that was supporting Younis's legs. Its head swung somewhere behind me, and in its fright, it lunged at Badr standing close. Badr fled: Younis toppled from my shoulders, knocking me to the ground, where we lay mixed up with the python.

The unfortunate snake, now really upset, struck out forcefully and fastened its jaws on my forearm, but Younis grabbed it by the tail and it let go again, turning on him. He hastily released the tail but while its attention was focused on him, I caught it round the neck. The indignant reptile, battling for its life, struggled fiercely in my grip, winding its tail round my leg and pulling so hard that it almost freed its head; I had to grasp tightly with both hands to maintain my hold and I was afraid that it would dislocate its bones. I yelled at Younis to unwind the tail from round my leg. Fortunately he had enough presence of mind to obey this instruction, and once the tail was free the python was unable to exert any leverage and the struggle was over.

In single file we carried its twelve feet back to the Land-Rover: I held the head in a loose grip in front of me, resting the body over my shoulder; Younis walked behind me, holding the main portion, while Badr, carrying the tail, brought up the rear.

This was one of the very few pythons I have seen that made any serious attempt to fight for its liberty, but the circumstances of the capture were such that it had little option. This python eventually became very docile, and was one that I finally presented to the Khartoum Zoo.

*   *   *

I think the python that caused me the most anxiety was an eleven foot specimen I caught only a few years ago. There was nothing untoward in its capture although it took me an hour or more of hard work to secure it.

The python was seen swimming across a river and climbing up the bank. When I reached the place there was no sign of it, but we unearthed it from a hole in the bank where it had taken refuge. Torn, dishevelled, covered with mud and oozing water at every step, for I had had to dig away part of the bank to reach the snake and I had slipped down into the river several times, I carried the python back to my house. As all my cages and enclosures were full, I had nowhere to keep the new captive. The next day I was due to go on safari and would be away a week or more. I did not really want the animal, anyway, for I had only caught it to prevent it being killed by the local people who had discovered it. I might have taken it with me and released it somewhere in the wild, but this was not possible.

In the end I shut the snake in a spare bedroom before I left, giving it a large bowl of water, and opening all the windows (the wire mosquito gauze prevented the python from escaping), with strict instructions to my servants not to go near the bedroom. I knew that they would not dare to go in, anyway, but I wanted the word to go round to discourage any would-be thief who noticed the open windows. Everybody in the district would soon know that I had left a big snake to guard my house while I was away.

When I returned from safari, I went to see if the python was all right. I found the bedroom door open, and no sign of the animal. I called my servants who were most distressed, swearing that nobody had been in the room. There seemed little doubt that they were telling the truth, but it was a mystery how the snake had escaped if nobody had opened the door. I examined the latch which was working perfectly.

We spent half an hour searching the house, a modern, two-storey building, with metal-framed mosquito-gauze at each window, but the snake was nowhere to be found. There seemed no possible hiding place that we had overlooked, and the only conclusion I could reach was that it had left through one of the doors although these were locked and the servants said that no door had been left open while I was away. I suspected that this was untrue, but I still could not understand how the python escaped from the bedroom.

Together with my apprehensive gardener I poked around in the likely places in the garden without result, but a river flowed at the bottom of my garden and I imagined that the reptile had found its way there being unlikely to linger once it was out of the house. Satisfied that the python had escaped, I forgot about the matter.

Three nights later at about 1 a.m. I was awakened by a

crash downstairs. Burglar, I thought, as I got up quickly and quietly. The stone stairs gave no creak of warning as I crept down on bare feet. I took my torch but the soft moon glow was enough illumination so I did not switch it on. The stairs led to an enclosed veranda at the back of the house forming a passage between kitchen and the downstairs bedrooms. A French window from the veranda led to the sitting-room which had two ordinary windows also opening into the passage. I looked through the sitting-room windows. Nobody there. Stealthily I investigated the two downstairs bedrooms, the dining-room and the kitchen in turn. There was no intruder. The windows and doors opening into the garden were all locked or bolted. I went back into the sitting-room and flashed my torch round.

On the floor was a broken vase. I was really quite relieved to see this for it was a hideous thing given to me as a present. I swung the torch beam round and there, on a built-in book-shelf four feet above the ground was the missing python. I leapt forward just too late to prevent a row of books crashing to the floor. In the ensuing struggle to subdue the reptile and prevent more damage, it managed to curl its tail around the lead to the wireless aerial and pulled my portable radio to the ground. Once again I shut the snake in the spare bedroom.

Before I went to bed I unravelled part of the mystery. I still did not know who had opened the bedroom door in the first place, but I now realised that the python had wandered out and found its way into the lavatory; whereupon it had climbed into the bowl and disappeared from sight. A tell-tale trail of water on the floor showed that it had emerged only a short time before. Fortunately the reptile had not found its way into the cess-pit as that would have been the end of it, but it must have remained somewhere along the pipe for at least three days, perhaps longer, before making its appearance in the house once more. Probably the flushing of the lavatory on my return had activated it.

The next morning I found my servant contemplating in some perplexity the smashed vase, the untidy heap of books, and the cracked radio on the floor. He had not begun to clear up the mess, he explained, in case that was how I wanted them. As my house (this was before I was married) was always full of various animals, scattered books, specimens, papers, insects being bred in odd jars or tins, and other paraphernalia, and since he was always being reprimanded for 'tidying up' and losing things, his restraint was not open to criticism. I had a look at the python, but it was innocently sleeping under the bed.

I was due to go on leave to Britain in a few weeks time, so I made an arrangement with a friend some twenty miles away to look after the python when I left, for he was very keen to keep it. He promised to have a big cage made, but I had to keep the python until the cage was ready.

Later that morning I had a telegram informing me that I was to be honoured by a two-day visit from a Mr. Bumble. Some weeks before, Mr. Bumble had informed me that he might be coming, and I had foolishly offered to put him up, for he had kindly given me hospitality on two of my infrequent visits to the capital. Mr. Bumble was from the Secretariat and was a Senior Person. I did not know a great deal about Bumble, but I knew that he was very conscious of his dignity, did not care for animals, and could not abide snakes. I had some rearranging to do before he arrived that evening.

On my way back to the house from my laboratory, I was stopped by a group of excited children who pranced round my car shouting '*Njoka! Njoka!* (Snake! Snake!)'. I took one of them into the car and he guided me about half a mile up the road, the rest of the piccannins scampering behind almost invisible in the clouds of dust raised by the passage of the Land-Rover.

Twenty minutes later I was back in my house with another python, almost as large as the first. I put it in the back bedroom with the first one while I had lunch.

My servants had a busy afternoon. They had to clean the back bedroom, which, although smaller, was cooler than the front ground-floor bedroom, for Mr. Bumble. Before they could do so I had to remove the two pythons. There was the one I had put in the room just before lunch, but there was no sign of the original snake; it had escaped again although it had been there two hours previously. Once more we searched high and low without success, and once more it had undoubtedly disappeared into the lavatory.

There was nothing I could do about it. Bumble was due at any time, and I had to hide the other python as well as a black-mouthed mamba, a spitting cobra and a couple of other snakes I was keeping in special cages on the front veranda. Besides these, I removed numerous jars of pickled specimens, various live insects, a squirrel, a pangolin and other livestock. Fortunately I had let free a tame owl a few weeks previously, although this had the disconcerting habit of returning every so often and hooting indignantly for food just outside the door or window. Also most of my snakes were kept in special enclosures in the garden so they could not cause Bumble any qualms. The only place for the new python was in the front spare bedroom, and I only hoped the servants would keep the door closed and that Bumble would not go in by mistake.

Bumble was late, fortunately, and did not arrive until dusk; the servants had cleaned and polished, the animals were all out of the way, so I was more or less in a fit state to receive him. I had even discovered how the python had escaped from the bedroom. In its perambulations round the room it must have reared up against the walls and the door; the door handle was of a lever-type, so that a simple up and down movement operated the latch. The snake, rearing up against the smooth door, reached the handle which it found to be a convenient support, and its weight pushed the lever down so that the door swung open. There was, of course, no pre-meditation in the action, and it was partly accidental that the python eventually wandered through the open doorway. The door was balanced in such a way that when unlatched it opened about eighteen inches of its own volition, but a breeze would close it again. In both cases when the python escaped from the bedroom, the wind, which at this time of the year often came up in the late afternoon, must have blown the door shut after it.

Almost the first thing that Bumble required when he arrived was to visit the lavatory and to wash off the dust of the journey. There was unfortunately only one lavatory in the house. I listened apprehensively expecting at any moment to hear cries for help, for the missing python might decide to emerge at any time, but Bumble returned without comment.

We had a drink before dinner. 'Glad not to see any snakes

about,' said Bumble, 'afraid there might be. I can't stand the infernal brutes, myself. You chaps amaze me, playin' about with 'em. Still, I suppose you know what you're doing.'

'I don't keep them in the house,' I said, 'at least, not when anybody comes. Have another drink?'

'Not too much soda. I remember an odd fellow when I was in Nigeria. Bit of an outsider, really, but do anything with snakes; I met him at Keffi — or was it Bida? — can't remember now, it must be fifteen years, I suppose. Anyway, . . .'

We had dinner. Bumble decided to have an early night. I escorted him to his room. He had already mistaken his bedroom and entered the room where I had put the second python, but luckily he had not noticed the snake.

'I hope that you've everything you want,' I said, taking a quick look round the room and under the bed in case during dinner the elusive python had taken it into its head to come back. 'Er . . . you'd better use the bathroom first. I'll just have a look and see that everything's all right.'

I left him hurriedly and searched the lavatory, bathroom and passage carefully. There was no sign of the python. Relieved, I went back to Bumble who was fiddling about with his suitcase.

'Don't be too long in the bathroom. I don't want to hurry you but the lights go off in about ten minutes. We're a bit primitive here, you know.' The electric light was produced by a diesel generator that the watchman switched off each night at 9.30 p.m. unless especially instructed; this gave me the opportunity to hurry Bumble without seeming discourteous.

Bumble nodded. 'That's all right,' he said, removing his coat and tie. 'I know what it's like on these bush stations— spent a lot of my time in Nigeria on out-stations. Twenty years ago this would have been luxury.'

I did not tell him that for me it was the height of luxury, having only recently spent five years in a place that was cut off by the rains for several months of the year, where mail came once a month if I was lucky and the carrier survived, where electricity was unheard of, and where for months at a time I was the only European for two hundred miles.

'Pretty hot to-night,' he went on, 'of course, it got much hotter in Lagos.' I forbore to mention that it was now the cold season. 'I think I'll leave my door open to-night to get a breeze,' Bumble went on.

This was not what I wanted. If the python came out during the night it might easily wander into the bedroom through the open door.

'Oh, I shouldn't do that if I were you,' I said. 'You'll get the room full of mosquitoes; they're all over the house despite the screens, but your room was sprayed earlier and will be free as long as you keep the door shut.'

'I've got the net; they won't worry me. You should see them in Nigeria. I can remember . . .'

Bumble was being difficult. When he had finished, I said, 'Yes, of course. Well, just as you like, but don't say I didn't warn you. Well, if there's nothing else you want, I'll say good-night.'

'Good-night,' said Bumble.

A few moments later I heard him leave his room. The gush of water told me he had finished in the lavatory, and a few minutes later the bathroom door slammed. I came downstairs. Bumble's bedroom door was wide open, but there was no sound from his room. Before I went to bed I carefully closed the lavatory door which Bumble had left ajar, first flushing the lavatory three times to discourage the emergence of the python during the night.

I was just dropping off to sleep when I heard the gush of water from the cistern again. I looked at my watch: one o'clock. From the top of the stairs I heard the creak of the lavatory door and I could see a faint glow from Bumble's torch as he returned to bed. I found it difficult to go back to sleep. At last I dozed, only to jerk awake again without being aware of what had disturbed me. I listened tensely. From below I could hear a faint sound, like some metal thing being scraped.

In my hurry to get out of bed I tore my mosquito net. When I slept downstairs I never bothered with one, but upstairs the house was always thronging with mosquitoes and I normally used a net. I flung on a dressing gown and once more felt my way down. To my relief the lavatory door was still closed, and again there was no sound from Bumble. I opened the door very slowly, but it creaked loudly all the same. I must oil this damned door, I thought.

Inside the lavatory the python had vanished again, but I could see that it had been out because there were wet marks on the floor, and a tin of Harpic had been overturned and rolled along. I pulled the chain; waited a few minutes and pulled it again. The noise seemed ten times as loud in the middle of the night, and I was sure that Bumble would emerge. As quietly as possible I went up to his wide-open door and listened, but he was breathing heavily. Very gently I swung his door to, and latched it.

Back in bed I found that I was not alone; many mosquitoes had joined me; attracted by the warmth of the bed, they had flown through the hole in the net. I lit my lamp and killed them which took me quite twenty minutes. The light attracted every insect in the room, and there were hundreds. I tied up the hole in the net; by now, it was nearly 4 a.m. Outside I could hear the unpleasant eunuch-whining of thousands of mosquitoes as they delicately jostled and probed the mesh over the windows. I read until dawn, unable to sleep again.

'I hope you slept well?' I asked Bumble at breakfast.

'Not very well,' he replied. 'Never do in a strange bed.'

'I didn't disturb you, I hope? I had to get up once or twice in the night.'

'No, no. Heard you, of course. But I found it a bit warmish last night, and somehow my door closed. Funny thing, for there didn't seem to be any wind. To tell the truth I've a touch of gippy-tummy just now. Keeps me on the run a bit.'

I heard this news with some dismay. I spent a second sleepless night, but although Bumble rose several times, the python remained anonymous and Bumble left without realising his good fortune.

'Well, goodbye,' he said on leaving. 'Many thanks for your hospitality. It must be quite a pleasant change for you to see someone in this place. I remember, in Nigeria as a matter of fact, one station I was on, saw nobody for two or three weeks. Lonely life, that, at times. Well, I must be off.'

As the python had survived in its unusual hiding place, I hoped it would appear again, and I just left the lavatory door permanently open so that it could leave if it wished. There was no sign of it for the next three days, but during the next night it must have wandered about for although I was not disturbed, the next morning I found traces of water on the floor, a small table had been overturned and the tin of Harpic had been rolled along the passage. After that, two weeks went by without any token from it. I began to think that it must have found its way into the cess-pit after all and perished.

During this time I had various male visitors, although none stayed the night. Depending on the caller, I either told him to beware of a python when he visited the lavatory, or else said nothing and hoped the reptile would remain quiet. Those people I told usually preferred to wait until they were elsewhere before relieving their feelings.

A week before I was due to go on leave, I opened the cess-pit manhole, and poked a long pole up the pipe. There was no result and I gave the poor python up for lost. However, only two days before I left the cook came to me in a state of great agitation.

'*Bwana*, I can't get in the kitchen.'

'Why on earth not?'

'Your python won't let me.'

Sure enough, the giant snake had somehow reached the kitchen and was leaning its bulk against the outside door. I caught it, and that day took it together with the second python, which never discovered the trick of opening the bedroom door, to Tom who was going to look after them.

Soon after I returned from leave six months later I went to collect them. Tom told me he was furious as somebody had left the door of the cage open only a few days before my arrival, and both snakes had vanished into the surrounding bush. Maybe the python was cleverer than I thought and really could open doors when it wanted to.

Perhaps it was just as well that the snakes escaped, for during my leave I was married, and my wife endured enough shocks when she came to Africa without sharing her first married home with a pair of large pythons.

INDEX